FREEDOM OF THE SOUL
A POST-MODERN UNDERSTANDING OF HINDUISM

About the Author

The author read Western philosophy at University of London, and subsequently taught it at various universities abroad. Amongst his numerous academic publications, the following books in the philosophy of religion are most noted contributions to knowledge: *Individuality and Reincarnation* (1978), *The Philosophy of Non-Attachment* (1982), *Consciousness and the Integrated Being* (1991), *Ethics and Spirituality* (1998).

In India, he has been a Fellow at the Indian Institute of Advanced Study, Shimla, and held the Chair of Culture at North-Eastern Hill University, Shillong.

Tel: 011-2294206
E-mail: mmurari@indiatimes.com

FREEDOM OF THE SOUL
A Post-Modern Understanding of Hinduism

M.M. AGRAWAL

CONCEPT PUBLISHING COMPANY, NEW DELHI-110059

ISBN 81-8069-002-4

First Edition, 2002

Published and Printed by
Ashok Kumar Mittal
Concept Publishing Company
A/15-16, Commercial Block, Mohan Garden
NEW DELHI-110059 (India)

Phones: 5351460, 5351794
Fax: 091-11-5357103
Email: publishing@conceptpub.com

Dedicated
to

Mark and Manoj

FOREWORD

Dr. M.M. Agrawal's *Freedom of the Soul: A Postmodern Understanding of Hinduism* deserves to be welcomed for two important reasons. Firstly, it sheds new light on some of the important concepts that we find in Hinduism, such as those of the *Brahman, atman, jivatman, karma* and *freedom*. The author has also discussed at a deeper level the concept of *avtar*, the eternal entering the temporal. Secondly, the book contains illustrative citations from important books of knowledge such as the *Upanisads* as also from a vast literature concerning Hinduism.

The author's erudition is evident throughout the book, and what is more important is the author's lucidity in articulation and exposition. The book offers a new approach to the understanding of the spiritual contents of Hinduism, and it can be said that it is bound to provide a fresh stimulus to the development of Philosophy of Religion in the country.

2-02-2002
New Delhi

KIREET JOSHI
Chairman
Indian Council of Philosophical Research

PREFACE

Twentieth century has witnessed great advances in the sciences and social organizations. But it has also witnessed great upsurge of violence causing great sufferings and sorrows to mankind. There is violence at all levels of our existence: between individuals, between groups and between nations. At all levels social entities are competing with each other for economic and political domination. Excessive wealth and power in one place is bound to create deprivation and alienation in another, resulting in all forms of violence.

The present generation is undergoing a huge transformation in cultural attitudes, in his way of life, affecting both his personal relationships and his 'living together' in a community. We have almost ceased to derive happiness from caring and sharing, and from creativity without the motive of personal gain. Personal success focused on promoting oneself, ruthless competition and acquisition of endless power, wealth and fame have become the norm for a good life. Social systems that are supposed to protect the freedom of the individual and promote the blossoming of the humanity in him, have turned so repressive that the individual sees no option but either to succumb to or to revolt with violence. Unfortunately, neither strategy yields the desirable human good: the peace, the harmony, the ending of isolation and alienation.

It seems to me that towards this end Hinduism has a great contribution to make. From the start, it is worth noting that even in the present climate, where 'organization' and 'collective action' are the *mantras* for success, Hinduism is probably the only religion which all along has retained its 'non-organized' and questful character. It is non-organized in the sense that its beliefs and practices are not subject to censor or endorsement by a hierarchical authority *in respect of their truth and morality*. The reason for this lies in both the structure and philosophy of Hinduism.

Structurally, Hinduism does not hail from some *one* book, the holy book for a given religion. This has the advantage that it avoids to stand for a closed system of beliefs. In Hinduism there are several books that are considered as sacred scriptures. No doubt, the *Gita* has come to be described as a holy book, but not because the whole of Hinduism is derived from it, but because it is believed to be a record of the words spoken by the Incarnate—God himself. Moreover, it is a book which shows the importance of retaining the older religious beliefs by providing them their proper place in the total scheme of Hindu spirituality. Furthermore, it introduces for the first time to the mankind the most profound truth of the incarnation of the personal God into the temporal world. The incarnation is supposed to occur at different times at different places according to the need of the world, thus maintaining the possibility of fresh interpretations of the Truth to be assimilated in the existing faith. The Hindu doctrine of Incarnation has ensured the element of structural openness in the religion. In this way also, it seems, that the post-modern understanding of the role of 'interpretation' in understanding a text has always been (though unconsciously) respected in the Hindu tradition.

In its philosophy also, Hinduism undermines all attempts to become an organized religion and suffer the evils of dominance by the clerics as well as by the self-styled defenders of the truth and the morality of the faith. In this regard the *Gita* is the best example of the syncretic character of Hinduism, whose teachings have rightly become the core of main stream Hinduism. It comes from the fact that Hinduism puts emphasis on the personal experiential knowledge of Truth. Its very goal of *moksha*, the final liberation or freedom of the soul, depends ultimately on the first-hand perception of the Truth by the believer. At all levels of human existence, it is the truth that frees him. By the grace of God one comes to know the Truth.

In its wonderful philosophy of action in the *Gita*, the Lord teaches us to act without attachment to personal successes, without fixing one's heart upon one's own gains from the acts he performs. On the other hand, the *Gita* warns us as well not to land into inaction. One has a duty to life and to society to act in the right way, according to *dharma*, the righteous order of existence, caring for the four supreme human goods of justice, compassion, truth and kindness. Without right action in life as a whole there is no hope of liberation. The impetus for right action, however, comes from the realization of the ontological interconnectedness of all things, all the forces of the universe and of all living beings, in an all-inclusive divine reality, the *Brahman*. It is this realization that finally ends alienation and conflict and generates in the individual a sense of responsibility for the whole.

In the contemporary world where man is given to the pursuits of the mind, to fragmentary action, to making compromises with evil for personal successes, to self-seeking egoism, he must turn to himself to discover what this self really is. Without knowing who and what he is and how he is related to Being, without appreciating, that is, the beauty of the integrated beingness of humanity, the endless mad activity for the pleasures of success, surely, has no meaning or ultimate significance. A good life must be anchored to Truth: the truths of the self, God and reality. Man must choose between living the life truly of a human being and living the mechanical existence of a conditioned conformist mind which is ignorant of the true nature of his own being. By encouraging self-knowing and ending alienation through 'freedom-in-God', Hinduism provides the radical solution to the ills of the modern society. In this regard Hinduism transcends the strict bounds of the rituals and rites and the social practices prescribed in particular religions. It amounts to a spirituality which is perhaps at the heart of all great religions of the world. Without the holistic action of this common spirituality there is little chance of peace within the individual and harmony in the society. A proper appreciation of Hinduism gives man the opportunity to reorient his life with courage and confidence and turn to his own spiritual resources to create a society in which each can live creatively and move steadily towards the goal of freedom of the soul.

M.M. AGRAWAL

ACKNOWLEDGEMENTS

I am grateful to Professor S.C. Malik for reading the manuscripts and discussing his valuable comments with me, and to Dr. Sukrita Paul Kumar for discussing the title and other editorial matters of the book.

M.M. AGRAWAL

CONTENTS

1

INTRODUCTION

> Wisdom comes to the man
> who meditates on Truth
> and lives and acts according to
> the correct eternal laws of Nature.[1]

The core of Hinduism consists in the belief in an eternal indestructible divine Reality, which has to be accessed by the individual self in religious action, upholding the access as the ultimate goal of human life. This access to the Eternal is conceived as the complete and final FREEDOM for the soul, which is implicated in the natural order of existence and the consequent rounds of births and deaths in the world. The whole of modern theistic Hinduism is an attempt to make this theme religiously intelligible and existentially realizable through a spiritual discipline which is so flexible as to suit any normal human temperament and any set of social and natural conditions. The *Bhagavad Gita* is the earliest and the most profound source of the monotheistic, Incarnation-centred Hinduism. It was written around 500 B.C., and its doctrines had travelled to the Semitic world, perhaps influencing the Christian faith in the Incarnation of Christ. Its scientific reasonableness and philosophical temper are especially significant for the religious mind of the present age.

Today the question of spiritual freedom is far more challenging, because everywhere in the world the forces conditioning our minds into what to think are getting stronger. We have an environment which is ruled by the deterministic science and authoritarianism. Not only in political, social and economic spheres, but also in religious and spiritual thinking, there are 'specialists' telling us what to believe. Then there is the media, the cinema and so on, constantly bombarding the human mind with materialistic values and propagating their own superficial understanding of what is important and urgent in human life. Under enormous influences of various forms of the inner and outer compulsions, man is forgetting the significance of 'spiritual freedom' and the importance of finding out the Truth for himself. Hinduism meets this challenge squarely.

Hinduism, at heart, is a religion of quest. One has to act to translate its teachings into a living experience of freedom and divinity. One cannot simply go through the motions of worship of God, or the gods and attend, mechanically, to the rituals and the rites prescribed in the brahamanical canons or the *Vedas*, and claim to be a Hindu. One has to choose to move steadily, through self-knowing and devotion to God, towards the goal of *moksha* or liberation from the constraints of *karma*, that is, from the inner compulsions due to the 'merits' and 'demerits' accumulated by the moral nature of works in previous lives. The Hindu has thus to live his life actively with the positive aim of achieving total freedom from the cycle of rebirth. He has to be sensitive to the performance of his duties (*dharma*) in the community, with sound judgement and compassion engaging in fulfilling actions but without the desire for reward of personal power, fame and wealth. The Hindu life is constantly guided by the supreme ethical principle of 'impartial treatment of all' and the *karmic* principle to the 'permanent possibility of improvement' of one's social and spiritual status in this very life. The pleasures from success in works, which naturally come to one, should be taken not with pride but with a sense of gratitude and the pains should be taken in one's stride. Constantly aware of the sacred nature of life, alive to one's social responsibilities and sensitive to the divine presence in the world and 'in the hearts of all beings', the Hindu engages with life in the spirit of a creative quest of the ultimate Truth. To present Hinduism as merely a religion of a passive acceptance of a 'faith' and a routine observance of the 'fixed' duties of each caste is to deprive it of its most distinctive feature of the active quest of *moksha* and the moral life that goes with it. This much is clearly stated in the *Gita:*

> So work, always judiciously
> Action is always better than inaction
> You cannot even keep your body
> alive without working.
>
> But works done for personal glory
> keep you in bondage to *sansara*
> So work without attachment (to its fruits)
> Always in the spirit of Duty.[2]

It is the religious character of the whole way of life required by the quest that eventually delivers a Hindu from the miseries of the chain of births and deaths in the world into 'the first and last freedom' of the spirit.

Hinduism is essentially holistic in approach. And the truth of any of its central doctrines is relevant to a fuller appreciation of the truth of the 'whole'. Thus, in Hinduism, the roles of worship, meditation, contemplation and enquiry are equally valuable. The Hindu prays to the Lord with the understanding of the inter-connectedness of all things (a relatively recent realization for the scientific world). He meditates and enquires into the truth that his inner-most being, his *atman*, the soul, is immortal and indestructible; it is of the same essence as the eternal *Brahman*, the ultimate Reality which is of the nature of Being, Consciousness and Bliss. He surrenders to the Lord, the *Ishwara*, with the realization that it is his own ignorance of the true nature of the soul, the world and the Divinity that keeps him in bondage to the implicate order of the *sansara*—the temporal world of works and its results, of births and deaths, of desires and attachments. He attunes his soul to the universal divine Spirit in total faith that the Lord will illumine him with the spiritual knowledge with which he will surely swim across the ocean of the troubled *sansara*. And this, indeed, is the promise of the Lord:

> With compassion towards the seekers (of God)
> With the light of the lamp of knowledge,

> Situated in their own hearts,
> I dispel the darkness of their ignorance.[3]

Even surrendered to the majestic omnipotence of God, in pure humility, the Hindu lives his life in the spirit of sacrifice and love for the creative enjoyment of whatever an honest living has to offer to him. He has firm faith in God's gift of the spiritual potential implanted in all human beings for their constant moral improvement towards the goal of *moksha.*

Hinduism is a religion of great optimism. It tells you that one's spiritual destiny is in one's own hands. For, its law of *karma* teaches that 'you reap as you sow'. And its law of rebirth teaches that even if one has not been able to make it in this life, he has hope, for if he has lived rightly he has the next life better suited for his further advancement. But, of course, if you lose sight of the ultimate goal of *moksha* itself and choose a way of life discordant with it, indulging in the temptations of the worldly gains, then you are surely doomed to get more and more entangled in the pursuit of pleasures and the consequent sorrows of the *sansara.*

It is a great pity that the most sensible and rationally defensible 'law of *karma*' has been presented as a blindly deterministic law. It has been often invoked to justify oppression of those who were born in poverty or in low caste. This is a total distortion of the meaning of *karma.* Surely, the law of *karma* does purport to explain why initially a child may be born in poverty or in a lower social strata in a given society. But that does not, by any means, exonerate the community from its moral responsibility of providing for all the opportunities to the deprived to be able to improve his lot. Nor does it justify the attitude of the privileged to look down upon the deprived. On the contrary, if the message of the law is correctly read, it becomes the duty of all to create an equitable social order which ensures the availability of 'opportunities' for the under-privileged. There is no limit to what an initially born-deprived can achieve in his life, including the ultimate goal of *moksha.* Nor is his initial resourcelessness any reason to believe that he is destined to remain that way for the rest of his life. On the contrary, freedom to improve one's lot is built into the law of *karma*. We will see in the relevant chapter how such freedom is not only fully compatible with the *karmic* determinations, but also necessary to its operations.

In the same vein the doctrine of rebirth has also been abused through misinterpretation of its import. It has been suggested that the belief in the chain of rebirths tends to encourage moral laxity and pleasure-seeking. For, one tends to think that one will make up for his present indulgences in the next life. To say the least, it makes the believer less concerned with the central pursuit of the quest of *moksha* and consequently less responsible towards his duties, which are thought of only as the necessary ingredients in the quest. This may be so. Man tends to ignore the urgency and postpone doing things which require mental discipline and which are not immediately necessary for survival. All the same, it is not the fault of the doctrine of rebirth. It is the fault of not reading the doctrine of rebirth along with the doctrine of *karma*. The neglect of one's moral and spiritual responsibilities now can only leave a man much weaker and even less disposed to the Spiritual in the next life. The 'postponement' in question can become a major retrogressive step for the next birth. Hinduism teaches that if you have faith in the wisdom of the sages and live your life according to the advice of the holy book of the *Bhagwad Gita*, you are sure to move steadily towards the Divinity and attain, by His grace, the final state of eternal freedom.

Hinduism is a religion five thousand years old. And during this span of history a vibrant reflective culture has been constantly adding to its wealth of spiritual understanding. For the same reason too, it has produced a variety of philosophical views on religious truth and a number of different approaches to the realization of the ultimate Reality. In the last chapter of this book we discuss four different ways—Contemplation, Action, Devotion and Knowledge—to find God and to enter the abode of the Eternal. The practicality and the correctness of this classification is most evident when one realizes that different human personalities naturally tend to find one or the other of the ways more agreeable to their specific nature. At the same time it has to be remembered that the difference between the "ways to God" is only a difference of focus and emphasis. They are not to be treated as mutually exclusive. Each has to carry the elements of the others along the holistic movement of an integrated religious discipline. Similarly, the Hindu variety in philosophical views matter only as long as one is confined to the area of discursive thought. But as one moves into the area of their specifically soteriological import, one gathers a remarkable unity of vision. In the end, they all maintain that the realization of *moksha*, the eternal freedom of the soul, is the highest religious achievement for man. And they are all committed to the belief in one divine Reality and its self-manifestation in one Supreme Being. And they are all equally committed to the belief in the law of *karma* and rebirth, the doctrine of incarnation and the wisdom of the manifold approaches to attain an existential access to the divine Reality.

Hinduism is the first religion of man which has proposed the doctrine of *Avatara* or the incarnation of God in the world of human beings. It is not a mere hypothesis, its truth has been ascertained in the *yogic* experiences of numerous sages. According to the doctrine, the Eternal enters into the temporal, God is born in the world of the humans to save them from the clutches of some great evil threatening to destroy the entire fabric of the righteous social order in some advanced society. God brings the Truth to mankind and shows him the way to its experiential attainment. He tells us:

> The ignorant do not recognize Me
> in the human form, and foolishly ignore Me,
> but those who have faith in God
> regard Me as the supreme Lord of all.[4]

And surely this doctrine makes great sense, when one considers the fact that the logical gaps to be bridged in the human understanding of God—between the temporal and eternal, the contingent and necessary, the immanent and transcendent etc.—are so bewildering and even incomprehensible that man would have never grasped the truth of the Divinity and his own spiritual destiny unless God himself, by his own example, by incarnating in the human form, were to demonstrate the possibility of his simultaneous immanence and transcendence. The Incarnation also confirms the possibility, as envisaged in Hinduism, of man becoming one with God while still living on earth, thus attaining *moksha*-consciousness even before his physical demise.

Again, Hinduism is the only religion which successfully resolves the conflict perceived by all religions, between the notions of a suprapersonal divine Reality and the notion of a personal God. Other religions also recognize that the true essence of God is beyond the grasp of the human mind. But they tend to assimilate this aspect of "ineffability" with a vivid description of the personality of a personal God. They fail to explain how God, when truly unknowable by the human mind, can be conceptually represented as a person at all. Hinduism reconciles these opposing perspectives upon God by treating the personality of God as a spontaneous act of self-manifestation of the supra-personal divine Reality. The personal God, Hinduism explains, is the best that the human mind can imagine when contemplating the causal power of the ultimate Reality in respect of the temporal world. And such a God, it claims, must exist. God's existence is required by the fact of the human presence in the world. The human being is unique in being a unitary source of three incommensurate forms of energy—material, mental and spiritual. Yet, man is a contingent being. He, therefore, requires a non-contingent Being who is at once the 'source of all energy', in the form of a personal God, to constitute him.

In Hinduism, both ways of looking at the divine Reality are considered necessary for a complete understanding of God, Further, Hinduism represents the personality of God in its embodiment, in human-like form. And this way of representing the personal God also makes great sense. For, surely, we are disposed to ascribe the predicates of human relationships (such as of love, compassion, mercy, grace, etc.) to the personal God to be able to relate to Him in a meaningful way. But these predicates are essentially intelligible only in behavioural contexts, involving embodied spirits like human beings. It makes no sense, I think, to talk of an abstract entity that it is loving, compassionate or merciful. All these predicates have evolved in human language, in the context of human relationship, and are ideally applicable to human beings. If we wish to extend their application to God, as we must do, then we must imagine His personality as embodied in a human-like form.

In this work I defend all the central doctrines of Hinduism as most "reasonable". Reasonableness is the most respectable epistemic category in philosophy today. It is located in between the two extremes of mere 'faith' and strict 'logical proof'. The degree of reasonableness is arrived at by assigning paradigmatic significance to the wisdom of the sages expressed in beliefs which have stood the test of time, and evaluating the doctrines in question in terms of their consistency and coherence with the former.

Hinduism raises the question of the meaning of life. Are human beings just work-machines and intellectual computers who must go on running after pleasure, or more and more money and power to keep them in a comfortable position? Hinduism observes that even the most materially successful man is one day struck by disability or depravity or old age which renders his pleasures and possessions utterly meaningless for him. The race for more and more pleasure does not lead to true happiness, for, throughout his acquisitive exercise, man is surreptitiously aware of his own emptiness and the impermanence of whatever he tends to identify himself with. Furthermore, he is aware of the inevitable death which finally cuts him off from everything he considers his own and renders the life of constant 'achievements' a totally meaningless enterprise. Man has to live his life in constant fear of his eventual nothingness without having come to know of who or what he really is. Hinduism observes that the meaning of life must be something which is ultimately an end-in-itself. This end is true happiness, beyond the familiar human happiness which is derived from ephimeral successes and occasional pleasures in a largely mechanical existence. Hinduism maintains that man is capable of attaining this happiness in this very life through any of the 'ways' mentioned above. It maintains that happiness is the natural state of the soul which has freed itself from the illusion of its identity with the body-mind complex and has realized its true identity with the infinite Being, Consciousness and Bliss. The ways of Hinduism help you to liberate your holistic intelligence from its earth-bound time-consciousness and find that 'wholeness' of being which we are all really looking for, but foolishly in our fragmented materialistic ways. The spirituality of Hinduism is the integrating power of self-awareness which directs the physical, the emotional and the intellectual energies to move together in harmony.

All in all, Hinduism is a religion where philosophical reflections have found validation in meditations and the devotional and contemplative spiritual illuminations of numerous *yogis* and sages. Fundamentally, it is a religion which encourages the individual 'to find out' for himself. It is not a religion of mere faith in the 'revelations' to some particular person, or written out in some particular book. To appreciate the deep meanings of its central doctrines fully, the reader must try to approach them with purity of heart and mind, in personal emotions, intentions and attitudes appropriately directed towards God,[5] man and the whole Nature visualized in their sacred inter-connectedness. Let us now see how Hinduism unfolds the great secrets of human existence and gives us the wisdom to conquer ignorance, fear and death in the realization of the highest spiritual state of "Freedom-in-God" or *Brahma-Nirvana.*

> In all beings that are subject to death
> One who sees the Indestructible God
> Equally effulgent,
> He alone truly knows Him.[6]

REFERENCES

1. *Rig Veda*, 10.47.6.
2. Ch. 3, 8-9.
3. *Gita*, 10, 11.
4. *Gita*, 9, 11.

5. The earliest mention of a personal God conceived as the creator is found in the *Atharva Veda* which is dated anywhere between 1500-2500 B.C.

   "The perfect One, the Creator
   possessing perfect power
   the life-giver to the perfect universe
   May we comprehend this perfection
   the giver of life to all beings". (15.29.5)

6. *Gita*, 13, 27.

2

TWO CONCEPTS OF GOD AND THE DEVAS

One popular misgiving concerning Hinduism has to be cleared right in the beginning. It is generally projected by the adherents of the Semitic tradition that Hinduism upholds a belief in many gods. This is completely false. At least since the time of the Upanishadic writings (1000 B.C.) and the time of its most clear presentation in the holy book called *Bhagwadgita* (henceforth simply *Gita* 500 B.C.), Hinduism has advanced a very firm faith in the monotheistic tradition of ONE personal God, akin to the God of Christianity, along with a belief in ONE impersonal ultimate Reality which is considered divine in nature and worthy of religious contemplation.

In the Hindu faith the personal God is considered to be the Supreme Being (the universal Person called *Paramatma*). This renders the very idea of 'many gods' illogical, for there, logically, cannot be several Supreme Beings. Hinduism holds no brief for such irrational fancies. In the *Gita*[1] Arjuna underlines the belief in one Supreme Being when he prays to the Incarnate-God Krishna:

> You are the original divinity, the eternal Person
> the ultimate Ground of the manifest world.
> You are, the omniscient one,
> the ultimate object of knowledge worth pursuing,
> You are the transcendent and the immanent,
> and the whole world is imbued with You.

But there is another much older conception of God. We find it in the *Rig Veda*,[2] which is perhaps the most ancient scripted religious document of mankind and the most holy source of subsequent Hindu philosophical reflections on religious doctrines. A categorical belief in the subsequent monotheism is anticipated in a famous verse in this earliest *Veda*, which maintains that the many gods, presiding over the powers of Nature, are to be considered only as some fragments of "the one divine Reality". It is this 'one divine Reality' that has come to be represented later as the Supreme Being without, as we will see, abandoning the belief in the ultimacy and the divinity of the one supra-personal Reality. In this conception, God, later addressed as *Nirguna Brahman* (i.e., 'attributeless Being'), is considered to be the ultimate supra-personal reality—the source of all manifest energy. But by 'source' one is not to understand a single individual substantial entity, distinguished from other separate individual entities and seated as it were at the geometric centre of the cosmic reality. By 'source' is meant rather the 'inner most' essential nature of the cosmic reality (in a sense, perhaps, in which H_2O may be seen as the source of water and electrons as the source of H_2O, and so on).

Nirguna Brahman, as noted earlier, literally means 'attributeless Being'. But in the Indian religious literature 'attributelessness' is interpreted in two different ways: as 'insubstantiality' and as 'indescribability or ineffibility'. In Hinduism (in contrast to Buddhism) it is to be taken in the latter sense. Thus, in this second conception, God is considered to be the very essence of reality—the nameless 'qualityless' Being, or the Absolute, the ultimate Truth-Eternal. What is interesting about Hinduism is that it does not see the two concepts as contradictory to each other. Rather, both are seen as complementary to each other and, therefore, both are seen as essential to the unity and the intelligibility of the doctrines central to Hinduism. But before I proceed to explain the meaning and importance of the two concepts of God in detail, I wish to spend a moment of reflection upon how the misconception of the 'Hindu belief in many gods' might have arisen.

There are two main sources of this. The first is the Hindu theory of 'representation' of the powers of God. In this context God's relation to the world is conceived under three different roles: as Creator, as Sustainer and as Destroyer. Since the Hindus believe in a cyclic order of existence, they believe that a time comes when life in the cosmos together with its physical reality comes to a total halt and dissolution, returning to its primordial origins whose nature is inconceivable by the human mind. This 'coming to an end' of the cosmos is accomplished by God's power as a manifestation of God's will. The deity who plays out this destructive role is called *Mahesh* or *Shiva*. But it is the same God, the only one, who has played the role of creating the universe in the first place. This Creator-God is called *Brahma*. Similarly, the God who plays the role of looking after, or by his power sustaining his creation, is called *Vishnu*. Again, it is the same God, who is otherwise addressed in common as ISHWARA. Thus, the Hindu trinity of *Brahma, Vishnu* and *Mahesh* is ontologically no different than the one *Ishwara*, who is represented in his three different cosmic roles of creation, sustenance and destruction. However, a further complexity is added to it by the Hindu practice of presenting these representations in human-like forms. Thus, the three deities of the trinity are drawn or sculpted with three different faces and, ideally, in three different postures. Further, the three deities also have their respective female consorts. These are called *Saraswati, Laxmi* and *Parvati* respectively. According to Hinduism, even the anthropomorphic deities are not deemed complete if represented without the female principle. Thus, *Ishwara* is sometimes represented by sculpting a body which is half male's and half female's, called *Ardhnareshwara* (Note that the female consort is not the 'better half' but simply the significant half). In popular conception *Saraswati* is specially worshipped as the Goddess of Learning, *Laxmi* as the Goddess of Wealth and *Parvati* as the Goddess of Protection. The three generic forms of *Ishwara* and their consorts are further represented in a variety of symbolic forms, in one or the other aspects of their total personality and worshipped accordingly. At all times, however, they represent only aspects of the power of one Supreme

Being or *Ishwara* and should never be thought of as equal to or in competition with *Ishwara*. Sometimes the three faces of God are sculpted on one body and the whole figure is called *Trimurti*, literally meaning 'the three embodiments'. Later in this Chapter I will try to show how very sensible it is to represent the personal God in human-like form and how useful it is for the worship of the divine. For the time being, however, I turn to the other source of the misgiving in question.

The second source is the Hindu belief in the *devas* who are all represented in human-like forms and in English written as "gods", advisedly with a small 'g'. The propagandists, however, ignore the difference between the big 'G' and the small 'g' and run to the conclusion that Hinduism advocates the belief in many Gods. It is important to be clear about the nature of gods. Under no circumstances a god should be thought of as representing any of the three manifestations of the Supreme Being, the *Ishwara*. The Hindu gods are supposed to be the inhabitants of the heaven, which is a part of the universe and is accessible to all the very highly spiritually evolved souls after their death. It is also believed that many adept *yogins* are able to travel to the heaven in their subtle bodies even during their life-time on the earth. The heaven is not the highest religious achievement for the Hindus. The ultimate goal of Hinduism, as we will see in a later chapter, is *moksha* or 'eternal freedom' of the soul from its implication in *sansara* or the temporal world. The gods of the heaven are to be placed on a scale of unequal powers, relative to the strength of their respective spiritual achievements. On the highest level, the chief gods of the *Rig Veda* are represented as in command of the cosmic forces especially relevant to the human world. Thus, there is a god of rain, a god of air, a god of fire and so on. In the *Vedas* prayers and sacrificial rituals and rites are prescribed to be followed by those who wish to receive a blessing or boon from any of these gods. In modern Hinduism it is very rare to invoke any of these gods. The gods that are invoked now-a-days (as for example, *Hanuman*, the so-called 'monkey-god') are most likely to be those who are believed to have played an important role in the drama of life enacted by one of the incarnations of *Vishnu*.

However, in principle, in the Hindu cosmogony, there could be any number of *devas* or gods, since there are innumerable worlds, each with their own hierarchies of *devas* and *asuras* (i.e., devils).

It is important to understand that *devas* and *asuras* are ontologically no different from human beings. They have souls or *atmans* like human beings. It is because of the merit or demerit of their actions performed during their human existence that they have been promoted or demoted to the abodes of heaven and hell respectively. They are still subject to the laws of *karma* and rebirth. A god having exhausted the merits of his *karma* in the enjoyment of the heaven is subject to rebirth as an ordinary human being in an appropriate world. And similarly an *asura*, having improved his accumulated stock of merits and exhausted his punishments, is due to be reborn as a human being. As the *Gita*[3] states it clearly:

> They then, having enjoyed the vast abodes of heaven
> and having exhausted the merits of their actions,
> return to the land of physical deaths.
> In this way, even
> the doers of the works
> of the three orders of duties
> go round and round in rebirths
> chasing their lust and desires.

Let us now look at the distinction and the relation between the two concepts of God more closely. But in order to appreciate the wisdom of the Hindu view fully, we need to keep in mind a philosophical distinction between two types of concepts which in modern times the great German philosopher Immanuell Kant has drawn. This is a distinction between a "formal" concept and a "determinate" concept. Roughly what Kant meant by a formal concept is that a thing subsumed under that kind of concept could be thought of only in its most general outlines. The knowledge of a thing obtained from its formal concept would not enable us to locate the thing within the spatio-temporal framework within which we normally experience the world. By contrast a determinate concept of a thing enables us to assign empirically identifiable properties to the thing concerned.

Now the Hindu God, conceived as *Nirguna Brahman*, refers to a formal concept, while the notion of *Sagun Brahman* stands for a determinate concept. To the *Nirguna Brahman* the great philosopher-saint Shankara (the founder of the philosophico-religious system known as *Advaita Vedanta* or Non-Dualism) could assign only the formal properties of *sat, chitta, anand*, that is, Truth, Consciousness and Bliss respectively. And such characterization is surely correct. For *sat* simply signifies the being of God, or the truth that God is the ultimate reality. It does not tell us anything about the contents of that reality. And *chitta* or consciousness is surely not empirically determinable. Consciousness is not a thing which we can cognitively become conscious of. We apprehend it non-cognitively along with our straight-forward consciousness of things. It is surely a formal feature of the way of being in the world of beings whom we call conscious. Consciousness is the most illusive yet most significant feature of the spiritual reality in general. And again *ananda* points to the idea that God is the state of an extraordinary joy beyond all human happiness. Indeed, God's bliss is inconceivable by the human mind. It is not to be found in the day to day world of strife. This kind of bliss, therefore, constitutes only a formal qualification of God's nature. And it is certainly appropriate to God-nature. We know that all human beings want to be happy. But total happiness is never found in the world of temporal relationships. Moreover, worldly happiness has always the seed of unhappiness within it. This is not so only because such happiness is short-lived, but also because it is fragmentary, that is, obtained in one field of life against the neglect of the rest. Furthermore, it is attained only or almost generally through struggle and strife, often at the cost of other people's happiness. So the idea of Bliss-in-God is the idea of an ultimate happiness which is holistic and which is completely free from the constraints of struggle and internal conflict. In this, again, it represents only a formal aspect of the ultimate reality or the *Nirguna Brahman. Nirguna Brahman* is the God of apophatic theology, who can otherwise be described only as *neti, neti, neti*, i.e., as 'not this', 'not this', 'not this', where "this" in each case signifies a determinate quality. Hinduism maintains that all manifest beings, including the personal God (the *Adideva*), originally came from the Unmanifest, the *Nirguna Brahman*, and eventually, at the end of a cycle of existence, return to it. It is of this *Brahman* that later even the Buddhists have asserted:

> There must be
> the unborn, unbecome,
> the unmade and the uncompounded
> for if it were not so
> then no freedom could be asserted
> from what is born,
> become, made and compounded.[4]

Now, with regard to the the *Saguna Brahman* or the personal God, as already implied, it is said that He is the primeval and the original theophany of the unmanifest *Brahman* to the human mind. He is naturally conceived as the supreme Person. Why 'naturally'? It is because for the human mind 'person', as we know him in the world, features as the highest form of reality. And we consider him the highest form of reality for this reason. Firstly, a person is a combination of all the three fundamental forms of energy known to man: the material, the mental and the spiritual. In the Hindu belief the spiritual energy is classed separately from the mental energy. For, the spiritual energy is manifested through the human creative intelligence. Creative intelligence, by definition, signifies 'pure spontaneity' which in turn presupposes a kind of 'freedom from causality' which can properly be attributed only to the soul, and not merely to the mental which is gripped in causality. Then, in spite of these three forms of energy appearing so distinct to the human mind, the human person is known to exist as a unitary being—a being who can at once summon and command them to produce an integrated effect. Indeed he appears to be, in the miniature, a 'source' of all the three forms of energy, as though he were made in the image of the eternal *Brahman*. And so it is natural for the human mind to conceive of the Supreme Being in the same image and think of God as personal, as the *Ishwara* or the *Paramatman*. And God-the-Person is naturally endowed with all the attributes that man can possibly imagine, enhanced to infinitely greater proportions in comparison with the greatest of the men that is imaginable. *Ishwara* is the ultimate reality, the source of all energy, conceived under empirically intelligible determinate concepts. That is why, He is called *swayambhoo* or the 'self-become'. God-the-Person is the primary spontaneous manifestation of the *Nirguna Brahman*; He is not an 'effect' of some causal process antecedent of Him. God is the cause of all causes proceeding from Him. In other words, God-the-Person is the intellectual understanding of the ultimate Reality, when we wish to concretise the Absolute. It is of such God that the *Gita* speaks thus:

> The supreme Being, the supreme Abode
> the Person-Eternal, sacred Existence,
> the ultimate Truth
> Unborn, Everlasting and Divine.[5]

There seems to be an argument here amounting to a proof of the existence of a personal God. Starting from the fact of human presence in the world, which is unique and contingent, we are entitled to seek an explanation for it being thus and so. We have identified the characteristic features constituting the human uniqueness. It consists in the fact that "person" represents a unitary 'source' of all the three forms of energy known to man. But a person is not a 'self-become'. Whatever be the cause of the existence of this unique unitary being, it is clear that the cause must (at least) be the bearer of the same unique quality as the effect—the quality which cannot be analysed away reductively. The first cause must itself be a unitary being or the Person, constituting the original source of all energy. This must be in the form of the 'self-become' person, the Supreme Being or the *Sagun Brahman*.

Further, as a necessity of thought, the supreme Person must be drawn into the intentional nexus; that is, He must be brought to stand in a meaningful relationship with human life. This is so because persons are able to realize their personality only in interpersonal relationships. It is, therefore, natural for man to seek to understand how he stands vis-a-vis God, the eternal Person. And even further, as a person seeks another person, human beings quite naturally seek to enter into a personal relationship with the divine Person. It is natural to man to seek the ultimate relationship. It is not surprising, therefore, that human beings approach the formally conceived *Brahman* through its embodiment in the form of personal God. So prays Arjuna to Krishna in the *Gita:*

> O supreme Person! the Father of all living beings
> the Life-Eternal, the Lord of the *devas*
> O Lord of the universe! the self-knower
> tell me of Your immanence in the universe.
> O Yogin!
> in what ways and in what forms
> shall I meditate
> to know You in Your person?[6]

The faith in the reality of both forms of God (the *Brahman* and the *Ishwara*) is integral to Hinduism; though, in actual practice, in certain cases, a Hindu may bypass the worship of *Ishwara* and yet attain salvation, that is, reach out to the absolute *Brahman*. However, the belief in the existence of the personal God seems to be conceptually necessary, since, without this belief, it is hard to see how mankind could have had any communicable knowledge of the ultimate Reality in the first place. It is "*Ishwara*" that gives a determinate meaning to "God" in the first place. It is *Ishwara* who first and foremost reveals the God-head to mankind, either through the prophets or, rarely, through direct incarnation in the world of human beings. It is the *Ishwara* who is seen as full of the perfections of which some are accessible to the human mind in contemplation. It is only through such determinate knowledge of some of the perfections of God that the human mind can, with the aid of his understanding and imagination, comprehend the truth of the divinity at all. In any case, for most of us the *Ishwara* is the ultimate. For, most of us are unable to transcend the limitations of our own minds which are made up with determinate concepts. Our entire conceptual repertoire is grounded in one way or the other in our common experience of the world. And, it seems clear, that for most of us only when we have experienced *Ishwara* first (which is rare enough) that we have any hope of going beyond the determinate to the truly ineffable essence of the divinity. The *Gita* states this fact well as Krishna speaks:

> Of the multitude of human beings
> hardly few strive for spiritual perfections.
> And out of the striving ones
> hardly few achieve them.
> And out of those who actually attain some
> rarely someone knows Me in my true essence.[7]

How sensible is it to represent the personal God in the anthropomorphic form? And how useful is it for the practice of worship of the divine being? The answer to both these questions lies in the consideration of the very first step taken from the unmanifest *Brahman* to the intellectual representation of *Ishwara*. It is an amazing fact of religious worship that all the theistic religions of the world invoke both the concepts of God we have discussed, but in one breath, as it were. The sharp difference between the two is not taken note of. The two concepts in question are usually run through together without either explaining or justifying the shift from one to the other. All the religions invoke a common formal concept of God, but their determinate concepts can vary considerably. In the formal way God is identified with Truth-Eternal and the self-existent 'Source of all energy'. And then it is said that the essential nature of this Truth or the Source is beyond the grasp of the human mind, and therefore 'inconceivable' and therefore 'ineffable'. What is meant by the inconceivability in question is that the essential attributes of God cannot be brought under any determinate concepts such that God can be held in an empirically meaningful way in a spiritually significant relationship with human beings. It is this aspect of the essential nature of God which, as we have seen, Shankara has distinguished and explained so well under the idea of *Nirguna Brahman*. It is of this ineffable essence of God too that the *Kenopanishad* says:

> The eyes cannot reach it
> Nor can speech describe it
> Neither imagination, nor intellect nor
> understanding can perceive and know that Truth
> It is distinct from things known
> And different from things unknown.[8]

In the same vein the Islamic philosopher-saint Ibn'Arabi has written that when the human mind has knowledge of God, what he or she knows is an image of God, rather than the abyss of the divine being which lies beyond thought.[9] The point is that we cannot describe the eternal essence of God in terms of any such attributes through which we could possibly contemplate entering into a personal relationship with Him. Yet every religion does exactly that and Hinduism is no exception. For example, a beautiful such combined description of God is provided in the Sikh teachings as below:

> The One Transcendent Being
> He is Truth Eternal,
> He is the Creator,
> He is the Person all pervading,
> He is without fear,
> He is without rancour,
> He is beyond time,
> He is only the form that exists,
> He is unborn,
> He is self-existent,
> Through the grace of the *Guru* is He realized.[10]

Religion quietly slips into thinking of God in a determinate way. It makes an intellectually intelligible image of the eternal so that the temporal human mind can relate to Him: worship Him, pray to Him, place Him in his own spatio-temporal world in all sorts of ways. And this important first step towards a concrete determination of God is taken when he is assigned the status of a 'personal being'. His personality is then filled with a variety of empirically significant predicates, all of which are then interpreted in terms of human needs and aspirations: God is all merciful, forgiving, loving, all-knowing, omnipotent, our father in heaven and so on. The emphasis on one or the other attribute varies from sect to sect within Hinduism, just as in any other religion. In Hinduism, for some the personal God is not even the creator, in a self-conscious manner, of the universe. He is the creator only in the sense that originally every thing emanates from Him. And in another strand of thought, God is considered as the constant 'presence' of infinite power, goodness and beauty. And this presence is necessary and sufficient for the world to go round according to the eternal laws of Nature.[11] Generally, however, it is held that the personal God is the creator (as well as the destroyer and the sustainer) of the universe, and, given the purpose of giving God a determinate personality at all, his personality is best represented as embodied in an anthropomorphic form. So the answer to why God is represented in human-like form is simply that it is the most natural thing to do, once the inconceivable eternal essence of God has been given an empirically recognizable personality. Those who have read twentieth century Western philosophy, especially Ludwig Wittgenstein, would aptly understand that the anthropomorphic representation of personal God is not only 'natural', but also the most rational and logical step to take. It is so in view of the fact that the attribution of psychological predicates (such as loving, forgiving, etc.) to a living being or a person, is initially made intelligible only through their application in behavioural situations involving a body. Thus, Wittgenstein's famous gnomic apothem: "The human body is the best picture of the human soul."[12] That is, it would make no sense to ascribe predicates describing inter-personal relationships to a being who is essentially disembodied. Thus, Hinduism, with its typical philosophical bent of mind, could see no alternative but to represent the personality of God in its embodied form.

But now, it will be asked, how can the Hindu religious philosophy justify the "first step" (i.e. the movement from pure unmanifest *Brahman* to the personal God) in the first place? If the human mind can never grasp the true essence of the eternal *Brahman*, then how can it turn it into the personality of a personal God at all? And if it did, then wouldn't it be the case (as Ibn'Arabi noted) that the knowledge of God would only be the knowledge of his 'image' constructed by the mind? And in that case what would be the value of such knowledge? These questions are most pertinent. And in my view only Hinduism has answered them satisfactorily.

We have already alluded to the instinctive religious need of man of bringing the unknown into the known, the eternal into the temporal, into the intentional nexus. But a proper understanding of this, again, is provided by the great exponent of modern Hinduism, the Vedantic philosopher-sage Shankara. According to Shankara, the conception of the suprapersonal Absolute, the *Nirguna Brahman*, is an abstraction from the conception of the supreme Person. Human mind, he argues, cannot attach any sense to the idea of an 'inconceivable something', as distinct from mere 'nothingness', without first contemplating a 'determinate something' and then taking its specific, empirically meaningful, determinations away from it. And thus, in effect, Shankara reverses the order of what I have described as the "first step", of providing a personality to the ineffable Absolute. If this is admitted then it follows that the conception of *Ishwara* or the personal God is the very 'form' in which the Absolute can appear to the thinking mind at all. This means that the conception of *Ishwara* is the very fulfilment of the knowledge of the ultimate reality. *Ishwara* is the objectified-Absolute, and in that sense it does not represent just a mental 'image' of the Absolute, but rather the Absolute itself. *Ishwara* is *Brahman* as apprehended by THOUGHT. And in so far as THOUGHT is a characteristically human way of knowing any communicable knowledge, the knowledge of *Ishwara* would not only satisfy human religious aspirations, it must also be seen as the foundational ground for proceeding to acquire more abstract (though ultimate) knowledge of the Divine Reality.

All the same, it must be mentioned that Hinduism invokes another, a quite different and most significant, sense of "knowing". It is a sense in which the self-conscious mind is completely laid aside and its cognitive relation to the object of knowledge is totally suspended. In this sense 'knowing' becomes 'a way of being' in relation to God. This relation in its highest stage is the relation of epistemic identity, and generally for the Vedantic thinkers, even of the ontological identity. In this state the individual soul does not distinguish its identity from the identity of the cosmic soul or the highest divine Reality. In this state the subject-object distinction totally disappears:

> That which is the true essence
> and inhabits the whole universe
> as its Soul
> that is the cosmic Soul, the Reality
> and That art Thou.[13]

There is a strong tradition within Hinduism, known as *Advaita Vedanta*, which considers this way of knowing God as the highest religious achievement. But that, in no way, diminishes the importance of devotion to the personal God. Shankara's argument above makes it abundantly clear that the worshipper of *Ishwara*, in any of his forms (*Vishnu, Shiva* or *Brahma*), is not worshipping something imaginary. He is worshipping the *Nirguna Brahman* in the only possible way it can be worshipped, which is as the *Sagun Brahman* or the personal God. In the end we have the same Reality looked at in two different ways. But both ways of looking at that Reality are seen to be complementary in Hinduism. Even further, they are seen to be necessary to the constitution of a complete and integrated understanding of God.

Perhaps the epistemic predicament one faces here is parallel to the one we encounter in case of our understanding of the nature of consciousness. On the one hand, we have a direct, first-person access to consciousness only in a non-cognitive awareness of the fact that one is conscious thus and so. This is case of 'knowing as a mode of being', since 'knowing' is achieved here only in being conscious of consciousness. And this kind of knowing is ineffable too, for in this act of awareness we do not attribute any phenomenological properties to consciousness *per se*. On the other hand, in the third-person perspective, our access to consciousness is only through its behavioural manifestations. But for that reason, we do not consider the third-person perspective less important or less real. We consider both perspectives equally important for a complete understanding of consciousness. Though it must be admitted that it is not easy to integrate the two forms of knowledge. The Hindu claim with respect to our knowledge of *Nirguna Brahman* and *Sagun Brahman* is similar to it. Both forms of knowledge are necessary to a complete understanding of God. Perhaps the mystic in any religion understands this and puts it well, for example, in speaking of God as 'the outwardly manifest and the inwardly hidden'.[14]

REFERENCES

1. Ch. 11, 38.
2. I, 164, 46.
3. Ch. 9, 21.
4. *Udana*, 8. 3; trs. D.M. Strong 1902.
5. Ch. 10, 12.
6. Ch. 10, 15-17.
7. Ch. 7, 3.
8. I, 3.
9. Frederick Copleston, *Religion and the One*, Search Press, 1982, p. 106.
10. Harbans Singh, *The Heritage of the Sikhs*, Manohar Publications, New Delhi, 1983, p. 17.
11. See for example the works of Raman Maharshi.
12. L. Wittgenstein, *Philosophical Investigations*, Blackwell, Oxford, 1953, p. 289.
13. *Chandogya Upanishad*, 6, 10.
14. *Koran*, 57, 3.

3

THE INDESTRUCTIBLE SOUL
Atman and the *Jivatman*

> The great inborn self is undecaying,[1]
> Immortal, undying, fearless, infinite.

The founder of modern Western philosophy, Rene Descartes asked the question "who am I?" He followed a rather circuitous route to arrive at the answer. He rightly thought that if he could separate the essential from the inessential to his existence, he would have arrived at the correct answer and this he (wrongly) thought he could do by ascertaining what he could not logically deny as essential to his famous dictum "I think therefore I am". And from this he took a long step to the claim that "I am a thinking thing", i.e., a mental substance whose whole essence was 'thought'. Descartes' answer does not seem to be right. For surely, among other things, one can easily imagine oneself in a state of, say, depression which is an emotion in which no 'object' need be thought. However, Descartes' separation of the self from the body is certainly right, since one's knowledge that one is a subject of experiences is independent of one's knowledge that one is embodied. What Descartes did not realize is that this knowledge is not a matter of thought, which is an exercise of concepts. In self-reflexive awareness one has a direct intuitive knowledge that it is the 'self' of oneself who is thinking now and it is the same entity which has had all those experiences which one attributed to oneself. This would not have been possible if the self were a physical substance, since the qualities and properties of a physical substance are not available to direct intuitive perception, they must be found out by observation with the senses.

In a more sophisticated philosophical example one can imagine a person exchanging his body with another person and retaining his own identity. This could happen if two persons *A* and *B* decided to have their brains transplanted in the body of the other. We know that the brain is the physical container of all one's memories and other psychological traits. Then *A* with the brain of *B* will remember to be *B* and similarly *B* with the brain of *A* will remember to be *A*. This shows that *A* and *B* have been able to retain their identities without their respective original bodies. And this in turn shows that the self is not the body but something else.

Moreover, we say that 'I have a body' and not that 'I am a body', indicating that the body being a composite thing cannot be equated with a unitary centre of consciousness; the body is meant for the use of the self.[2] But now, we say the same thing about the mind as well. Contrary to the Cartesian outlook, we say 'I have a mind' and not that 'I am a mind'. And the mind is also a composite thing, made up of different categories of conscious states, sensations, desires, thoughts, motives, volitions, etc. And we also say 'I use my intellect, my mind to solve problems etc.'

The Hindu thinkers have been rightly impressed by the locutionary force of such statements and took them to be the indicators of the truth in this matter. Moreover, in introspection, we are only aware of the instantiations of the mental phenomena which we ascribe to a single entity, an "I" or the self. In recent philosophy, a whole complex structure of the mental phenomena centering on an "I" has come to be known as the 'empirical self'. But here we must not forget that the empirical I, to which we ascribe our experiences, is itself a mental phenomenon, a self-reflexive thought of oneself. The "I" is the object of consciousness and not the subject-self to which all the experiences, including the I-consciousness, should be ascribed.

Moreover, mental phenomena are 'introspectively' objective in the sense that introspection, as an exercise parallel to that of sense perception, turns experiences into inner 'objects'. Further, mental phenomena display a special kind of unity which itself is brought about only through the integrating power of subjective self-awareness. Such phenomena as memory and the sense of moral and psychological continuity in personal existence especially display this unity. And the reference to the pure subject-self antecedent to the (constructed) empirical self is supposed to explain the unity of mind as well as the identity of a person.

The distinctness of the pure self from the mind can be shown by another sophisticated philosophical example. We can imagine that medical science may one day make it possible to have all one's memories erased and have them replaced by another set of 'memories' obtained from a memory-bank as it were. Now imagine a person going through a surgical operation to accomplish this transfer, but all along remaining fully conscious and aware of the changes occurring in his mind. Throughout this exercise the person remains aware of him as a unitary centre of consciousness. Clearly, in this case we can say that from the beginning to the end of this exercise the person in question has retained his self-identity, though he has lost his entire mind and acquired a new set of memories. From this we are compelled to conclude that the subject-self (which remained conscious of itself throughout the exercise) is something completely different from the mind as well as, as has already been shown, from the body. In thought or introspection the subject-self always eludes us.

In Hinduism the pure self, called the *atman*, is a spiritual substance, distinct from both the mental and the physical substances. It is of this substance that the *Gita* declares:[3]

> Weapons cannot wound it
> Nor can fire burn it;
> Water cannot wet it
> Nor can the wind dry it.
> It is impregnable, indestructible, beyond
> Incineration, immortal, eternal, living forever.

In the *Kenopnishad* the enquiry into the true self is conducted as follows:

On whose initiation the thoughts turn to desired objects,
And the life breathes into the bodies.
For whom does the speech state (meanings).
For whom do the eyes perceive
And the ears listen?[4]

The above enquiry introduces a new dimension in relation to mental phenomena and places the *atman*, the soul, in a new epistemic context. The soul is no longer seen as a mere passive subject of mental states (like the non-human animals are), but also a source of purpose, meaning and rationality. The most important aspect of this observation is that the soul represents a being for which the sense etc. delivers the goods according to their respective powers. The *atman* is thus an end-in-itself, a being-for-itself. Indeed it is the presence of the *atman* that transforms the mental phenomena into experiences. Experience proper is in its essence always personal. That is why, we attach no sense (except in a metaphorical way) to expressions such as 'I am experiencing your pain', 'she is feeling his depression'. Experiences are to be distinguished from mere happenings. The latter are objective; they can be present in a psycho-physical entity 'unowned' or without appropriation by a being who is an end-in-himself, a being like the human being. Such happenings are going on all the time. The eyes are 'seeing' as long as they are open. But not everything 'seen' is noticed or attended to and recognized as seen. The talk of 'experience' is to give meaning to the expression "how a mental happening is just to this individual".

It is this feature of experience which, as we will see later, gives meaning to the Hindu idea of 'non-attachment'—the power to stand back from, or be a pure 'witness' to, the mental phenomena constituting one's empirical self. And it is this idea which the *Kenopnishad* expresses as: "He (the soul) is the hearer of the heard, the thinker of the thought, the speech of the spoken, the life of the living and the seer of the seen. . . ."[5]

What is meant by the expressions like 'the hearer of the heard', 'the thinker of the thought', etc. is confirmed in ordinary experience of everyone. We all realize that on occasions there is a sense in which one can stand back from the operations of one's own mind and adjudge subjectively "I am that", where "that" refers to the mental phenomenon with which one is normally identified, and "I" refers to the one who stands back. The one who stands back is the *atman* and when he sees himself as implicated in the mental phenomena, he is called the '*Jivatman*' i.e. the *atman* identified with a personality.

Thus again, we notice a 'double-aspect' theory of the soul, as we did in discussing the concept of God in the previous chapter. The soul in its aspect of its identity with the psycho-physical entity 'man' is the empirical self, called the *Jivatma* or simply *Jiva*. And the soul in its aspect of being the transcendental subject of all experiences, including the experience of the ego-centered empirical self, is the inner self called the *atman*. Again, the knowledge of both these aspects of the soul is essential to a complete understanding of the nature and function of the soul.

For, on the one hand, as empirical selves, souls are necessarily embodied and perform the function of transmigration in the cycle of rebirths. On the other, souls in their essential nature as awareness are declared to be all-pervasive and eternal and in its highest understanding the *atman* is declared to be identical with *Brahman*, the individual soul with the cosmic-soul.

> There is my soul seated in the heart
> Larger than the earth and its atmosphere
> Larger than space and all these worlds.
> Enfolding all actions, desires,
> All odours and tastes,
> Withholding the entire universe,
> It does not utter words and has no concern
> That is my soul within my heart,
> That is *Brahman*,
> In which I will merge
> When I leave this world.[6]

The inner self is not located in the body, it is neither born nor does it die, yet it is the subject of all the manifestations of the empirical self.

It is never born.
It never dies
It does not exist.
In the past, present and future.
Thus it is ever-present, eternal, primeval
It does not die in the killing of the body.[7]

Furthermore, like the *Nirguna-Brahman* the soul is also declared to be beyond THOUGHT and malevolence:

It is beyond the grasp of the senses and the mind
It remains unaffected by the impurities of desire.
So knowing it as such
Do not lament (the physical death).[8]

This conception of the aspectival duality of the soul is very specific to Hinduism, and it is also necessary to the understanding, as we will see in the later chapters, of the Hindu doctrines of *karma*, rebirth and salvation. It is important, therefore, to get a firmer grasp of it.

The soul is categorically declared to be indestructible and, therefore, immortal. Indeed, it seemed self-evident to the sages. For, how could the soul be destroyed if it hasn't been caused to exist in the first place? And it couldn't have been caused to exist, since it is presupposed to the existence of the body itself. The body, as we have seen, is for the soul. To the sages the survival of the soul beyond physical death is not a problem. It is rather the other way round. 'How could the body exist without the soul?' they ask. Nor could the body be the cause of the existence of the soul, for surely 'being cannot come from non-being'.

In order to go further let us approach the concept analogically to our ordinary concept of the self. The concept of the self, which we employ in our day to day life, is the concept of a special kind of subject of experiences. A contemporary analytical philosopher sums it up well in this way:

"The ordinary conception of the self seems to credit it with the following (interrelated) properties: that it is a simple invisible substance; that it is not ontologically reducible to other sorts of entities and their relations; that its presence is all-or-nothing; that its survival can consist in nothing other than its identity over time; that its survival is not a matter of degree (since it is simple in nature); that it is a mental concept whose essence is best revealed from the first-person perspective (it is to be seen first and foremost as the reference of 'I'); the fundamental property of the self, which underlies it and explains the others, is the property of being a simple substance apprehended as such in self-consciousness".[9] Now, we can see that 'the self as a simple substance' is to the very essence of the *atman*, except that we have characterized this substance as 'spiritual' in place of the 'mental'. But if this were the whole story about the self, we seem to be faced with a certain dilemma.

The problem arises when we try to unpack the notion of 'being the subject of experiences'. How exactly does the subject relate to its objects, namely, the experiences? When we look closely at the phenomenon of "having experiences", we find that in the moment of actually having an experience the self has (literally), 'become' the experience. That is, in the state of 'experiencing' the peculiarity of the 'subject-object' relationship is that it is a relation of identity. If I am experiencing fear, for example, I am my fear. I do not notice an ontological gap between me and my fear. It is not as though I am first aware of myself as a distinct simple substance, and then I attach fear to it 'externally', as it were. I am my experiences through and through. And in actual fact this is an ongoing process. I am never left alone simply with my pure 'self'. The picture of the self that appears from these considerations is that the self is a process of constant 'becoming'. And this surely undermines the picture of the self in its ordinary conception as a permanent unchanging entity in the form of a simple substance. Yet, it seems to me that both these perspectives (the substance-view and the process-view) upon the self have to be accommodated, and if possible integrated, in a complete account of the 'individual' consciousness. The Hindu conception of the soul does exactly that. By according it an inner nature, whose ineffable essence can be grasped only in a direct meditative intuition, it does justice to the ordinary concept of the self as a simple substance. While by determining its identity with reference to the psycho-physical entity, the *Jivatman*, it does justice to the phenomenon of 'being the subject of experiences'.

It is of these two aspects of the soul that the *Shvetashvatara Upanishad* speaks in the following verse:

> Of the two birds
> Sitting as close companions
> On the same tree;
> One enjoys the sweet fruit
> While the other watches in tranquillity.
> On the same tree
> A person sits in distress
> And dejection for his impotence;
> But when he sees the tranquil one,
> The Master self-satisfied in his glory.
> He is freed from his sorrow."[10]

Of the two birds referred to in the verse, the Master is the 'inner self', while the one that is eating the fruit is the empirical self, the *Jivatma*. In effect, Hinduism conceives of the soul truly in the image of God, who is considered as both outside the universe as the ruling Lord, and immanent as residing in the heart of all beings. This is surely most reasonable and the clearest account of the integration of the two aspects of selfhood in the light of ordinary human experience. As Krishna affirms:

> In the world of the living
> All living beings
> Are only my eternal parts.
> In the form of the *Jivatma*
> Which stimulates the five senses
> And the mind in Nature.[11]

And the complete picture of the embodied soul is drawn thus: "Know the soul to be the lord of the chariot, the intellect the driver and the mind as the reins. The sense organs are the horses. The *atman* is the owner of the chariot. Wherever the horses take it, directed by the reins, it needs must go. The key lies in the control over the mind and the right direction given by the intellect."[12]

REFERENCES

1. *Brihadaranyaka Upanishad*, 4.4.25.
2. Cf. *Sankhya Karika*, 17.
3. *Gita*, 2, 24.
4. I, 1.
5. I, 2.
6. *Chandogya Upanishad*, III, 14, 4.
7. *Gita*, 2, 20.
8. *Ibid.*, 2, 125.
9. Colin McGinn, *The Character of Mind*, O.U.P. 1982, p. 121.
10. IV, 6-7.
11. *Gita*, 15-7.
12. *Katha Upanishad*, 2, 22.

4

KARMA AND REBIRTH

> Though one may be tired of
> Repeated failures, let him begin
> His efforts again and again;
> For fortune favours the man
> Who perseveres in his undertaking.[1]

Perhaps the most fascinating and scientifically tempered doctrine of Hinduism is the law of *karma. Karma* literally means 'action' or 'law of action'. Simply stated it embodies the universal principle of cause and effect relationship, applied to human actions. We know that in the physical world everything is governed by causation. Each cause has its own specific kind of effect. If we put 'H_2' and 'O' together we will get water, not Coca-Cola. The law of *karma* is simply an extension of the acknowledged principle of physical causation into the intentional nexus. This is only logical. If causation is universal, to be truly so, it must apply to all kinds of events irrespective of the nature of their antecedent causes. We know that the human being is not simply a physical but a psychophysical entity. Man is a unique entity in that he is at once both physical and intentional. The existence of intention implies that human actions also have moral value. Human action could not exist without consciousness. This is because "action" is a hybrid concept. It includes physical movements as well as antecedent psychological states—the sequence of belief-desire-intention and will. Since human beings identify themselves with their choices and the will which executes them in the world, their actions naturally carry "merit" or "demerit" in moral terms as well. The law of *karma*, therefore, turns out to be a moral law as well, where the results of our actions embodying our own choices can be classified as good or bad in so far as they are determined by the moral character of our actions. In this way the law of *karma* sets up a chain of events in one's life where one effect enters into the set of causes for the next effect. Thus, all along, the chain of events is simultaneously free and determined. It is determined in so far as it has antecedent causes. And it is free because all along the chain the human soul is free to identify or not to identify itself with the antecedent psychological states constituting one's choices. If we are inadvertently led to identify ourselves with all the desires that arise in our consciousness, then we are ourselves responsible for their result. In common parlance this idea is expressed by saying "as you sow so you reap".

In Hinduism there is no sharp divide between the physical and the mental. The *karmic* causes include elements from both. The soul in itself is not subject to the spatio-temporal causation. The soul is declared, as we have seen, to be 'unborn, eternal, primeval and everlasting'. But the soul is implicated in the system of causation through its identity with the psychophysical biological entity, 'man'. It, therefore, suffers or enjoys in the world according to the law of *karma*. In principle, the soul is deemed free to wrench itself away from the 'personality' which is ascribed to it. Indeed, as we will see, that is the goal of spiritual perfection. That a soul does not affect this separation is considered to be its 'original choice', and therefore, its self-determination of the course of events to follow.

The law of *karma* operates in the entire chain of lives, of births and deaths, which an individual soul goes through until it attains the final liberation or *moksha*. Indeed, the law of *karma* would determine the lived character and the status of the soul in relation to the implicate order of the world. At the time of birth the accumulated merits and demerits of *karma* of the previous lives would determine not only the potential nature of the soul's mind and body, but also its location in the order of existence. This is only to be expected, since *karma* has to operate in the backdrop of both the natural and the social environment.

It is generally believed that the law of *karma* suggests a wholly deterministic outlook. That, as we have already indicated, would be completely wrong to believe. In fact, Hinduism is the only religion that has succeeded in providing a reasoned understanding of the simultaneous working of *karma* and the freedom of the will in the human life. In the law of *karma*, freedom and determination go hand in hand. On the metaphysical level it can be understood to mean that freedom is self-determination, where the determining factors in the 'self', i.e., the desires and the will etc., are themselves seen to have spontaneous origin in the soul. Since a chain of cause and effect has been spontaneously set in, our choices are self-determined in accordance with the law of *karma*. My birth to the parents I am born, therefore, itself becomes an act of self-determination. It is the merit and the demerit accumulated in the empirical self that naturally drives him to be reborn in a certain milieu. Similarly, morally too *karma* and freedom are reconciled. Where one is located in *sansara*, the order of existence, there one morally deserves to be. In the chain of births and deaths our choices are always made within a certain psychophysical framework in which our location is the result of our own earlier choices. An example of habit-formation may perhaps help us to imagine the human situation in this regard. We know that in case of habits, initially we quite freely create the conditions within ourselves, from which we subsequently feel 'compelled' to do certain things which we say we want to be free from. But the feeling of compulsion is just as much of our own making as the desire to be free from it. In principle, one is always free not to have chosen thus and so. But that freedom is not exercised due to the belief that we ourselves are the originators of our desires *ab initio*. Freedom is never exercised in a vacuum, there will always be some causal factors limiting our choices. But these factors cannot be called 'determining' in the sense of *binding* to one and the only course of action. The identity of an action depends on our intention, which one is always free to assent to or dissent from, inwardly. This one can achieve by the power of the "creative intelligence" present in the human soul—an intelligence which is not subject to the spatio-temporal constraints. It is a pity that we do not normally exercise this inner freedom and move along the path of *karma* willy nilly. But in reality one can always stand back from one's desires and compulsions. Indeed, it is a matter of common experience that we often do so quite successfully.

The moral dimension of *karma* clearly recognizes and firmly implants the principle of natural justice in the universe. Since all living beings are governed by *karma*, there is justice and moral order in the entire universe. And, since all living beings have relatively low or high degree of freedom-consciousness manifest in their choices, any misuse of the free will in causing suffering to others has to be accountable and punishable under the law of *karma.* The law of *karma* is the only account of the moral functioning of the universe that makes the presence of apparently unjustifiable suffering and evil in God's world wholly intelligible. We can understand the presence of evil in the world as the result of the free will of the wicked. But we are unable to understand why, for example, an innocent child should be suffering, or be born handicapped. The Hindu answer is that the sufferer is working out the effects of his own demerits of *karma* accumulated in his previous life. Similarly, it is explained that while a willful wrong doer exercises his freedom in choosing to do wrong to another, the victim, in fact, deserved it for his earlier *karma.* Thus, law of *karma* stipulates a 'pre-established harmony' between the choice of the villain and the deservedness of the victim. Nature has ordained things in such a way that the wicked are naturally attracted to perform their wickedness upon those who are deserving punishment for their *karmic* failures. That is, the wrong-doer chooses his victim for his own reasons and acts freely from his own desires, but the victim he chooses is already deserving of the harm for the reasons of his own *karma.* The wrong-doer is not making his choices under 'orders' from *karma*, he is a moral agent and not an executioner. *Karma* will hold him responsible for his free actions, independently of the fact that what he is doing fits in with what is required by another's *karma.* There is justice through and through. One should do one's duty irrespective of the considerations of what the other deserves on account of his *karma.*

The exercise of the natural justice should be left in the hands of *karma*. To give a *karmic* justification for one's wickedness is sheer irresponsibility and foolishness, for *karma* knows the truth and one will not go unpunished.

Nor does *karmic* determination lead to fatalism. Fatalism is the view that "what will be will be", so why shall I work to attain anything. But *karma* tells you that what will be will indeed be, but only through your own efforts. The role of free will may not be immediately obvious because the network of forces within which one operates is most complicated. But *karma* assures that one's own efforts will always make a difference (This is so also in Hindu astrology; the stars condition but do not compel). Personal moral responsibility, therefore, cannot be sloughed off on to the objective determinants of *karma*. Contrary to the popular objections, the law of *karma* puts firmly your destiny in your own hands. With *karma* there is every reason to be optimistic. In Hinduism there is no eternal hell or eternal heaven. Even if *karma* has send you to hell, the merits of your fresh *karma* will eventually pull you out of it. And similarly, you have to be responsible for your *karma* if you happen to be in heaven, for the demerits of your *karma* in heaven will surely bring you out of heaven sooner than later:

> They then enjoying the vast heavens
> When there merits are exhausted
> Return to this earth again.
> And in this way even the followers
> Of the three Duties (*Dharmas*)
> Remain entangled in the rounds of rebirth.[2]

This, however, does not mean that the law of *karma* renders the belief in God redundant. It is true that the law of *karma* operates independently of constant interference of the will of God. But it is an eternal expression of the will of God in the first place. It takes the infinite power and wisdom of God to make it operational in the world. Moreover, man's relationship with God and with others on account of God's presence in them is a sure way of improving one's *karma*. As we will see shortly, the merit of faith and surrender to God is so great that one is never lost on his path to the everlasting freedom. The law of *karma* puts the world in a proper religious perspective. It holds all mankind and all living beings within its fold. Its justice is equally valid even for the pagan. The atheist is only losing the extra opportunity to enhance the merit of his *karma*; he is not losing the opportunity to go to heaven, or to be born in a religious family in his next life, altogether. Indeed, the logic of the law of *karma* and the independence of morality from religious belief have led some Hindu philosophers to ignore the belief in the existence of a personal God. But this is not so in modern Hinduism. As already noted, the Hindu sees the law of *karma* as an expression of God's will in his total act of creation. And this is surely right. As God is merciful and forgiving, he has to find a way out for the non-believers and the wicked as well. In Hinduism, the way out is provided by the fact that the non-believer can be moral without being religious and the wicked can off-load his demerits in subsequent good conduct. This is a distinctive feature of Hinduism. Only Hinduism, through its law of *karma*, succeeds in explaining how God can be forgiving and just at the same time and how his Law has universal application irrespective of the faith of the individual human being.

It might be objected, however, that 'punishment' on account of *karma* is unfair, in that it can hardly count as 'punishment'. This is so because suffering inflicted upon the guilty to count as punishment must be against a clear acknowledgement of the guilt. This requires that the guilty must be aware of his guilt. And even if he, from his own point of view, refuses to acknowledge it as guilt, he at least has to know what the charges are against him. But in the case of *karma*'s dispensation of justice, *ex hypothesi*, the punished has no idea of what he is being punished for. In his previous life he was a different personality and in his present due to a different upbringing he may have shed the seeds of evil intentions altogether.

This defense of the sufferer, however, ignores some important aspects of the law of *karma*. Firstly, it has to be remembered that though the personality of the sufferer is different in this life, it remains a fact that he in a deeper sense remains the same person, for causally his self-identity continues. His case is then like the case of a criminal who after committing the crime undergoes a thorough religious conversion. He is still punished for his crime already committed, though with the promise of a 'reward' for his transformed condition after he has done his sentence. Moreover, spiritually such criminals are receiving the reward even as they go through the sentence; they are able to take their sentence in a good spirit, turning a vice into a virtue. Next, as far as the *karmic* sufferer's lack of knowledge of what he is being punished for is concerned, two points have to be made. One, that in Hinduism, it is, at least in principle, possible to know of one's previous lives. In *yogic* meditations it is possible to "recall" one's previous births. Alternately, though admittedly rarely, it is possible to learn of one's previous life from other adept *yogis*, or from astrology. Two, more importantly, that the suffering in my present life is wholly self-invited. My *karma* is not another person, a judge, who has to tell me what the charges are before he pronounces the sentence. I am already implicated in the order of the intentional world governed by the law of *karma*. Like an arrow, released from the bow, must find its way unless obstructed, my actions too must manifest their *karmic* merits and demerits unless overtaken by a higher *karma*. One can easily see the truth of this perspective in the familiar day to day life itself. For example, a man, who is initially tempted by small greed to exploit others and then to petty crimes, gradually promotes himself to a full-scale criminal. He is now unable to check his evil intentions. In other words, through his own temptations he has altered his character and determined the overall nature of his future.

But a much deeper justification of the 'deservedness' of the suffering due to one's *karma* is this. For this we have to consider how the sequence of the *karmic* effects is set up in the first place. Here, we may note that the Hindu counterpart of the original sin is the 'separation' of the *atman* from the one true self, *Brahman*.

> In the beginning
> before this universe

there was being (*Brahman*) alone
one without a second.
By the power of thought:
"Let me be many, let me procreate."
it all arose.[3]

The separation consists in the fact that the *atman* (which in its real state is ever abiding in *Brahman*) through the spontaneity of consciousness identifies itself with a psycho-physical instrument of action. As *Brihadaranyaka Upanishad* observes: The person is identified with desire. And as his desire so the operation of his will, and so is the action he performs, whatever action he does accordingly he attains.[4] And through this identification in turn, the soul is identified with a particular ego, which provides the subjective point of view for the *atman* upon the universe, signifying the process of the *atman*'s implication in the world-order. The *atman* then carries the pain of this separation all along its implicatedness in the life-world. But the overwhelming presence of the temptations offered by the ego occludes its return to the *Brahman*. It is, therefore, an unfulfilled duty to oneself to free oneself from this empirical self-identity and its desires, which separate him from *Brahman*. Now, so far the picture seems to me to be correct. Though it is a metaphysical doctrine it can be tested out by the presence of its implications intimated in day to day life. We all feel a sense of alienation from being and a sense of emptiness of the 'I'. The ego is what separates us from the rest of the existence. In the hearts of heart we are all longing for unity with being. But not knowing how to achieve this, we (foolishly) try to attain inter-subjectivity with God through extreme means, such as rituals and sacrifices. We are longing to end this separation and we express our failure to do so in what the existentialists call 'the objectless anguish and despair'. But some of us do also feel, if they are lucky, on rare occasions, the total absence of the 'me', as for example in a sudden encounter with something of stunning beauty. This is in common experience and the great artists vouchsafe for it when in their deeply creative processes they are 'lost' to their art—when the dancer 'becomes' the dance, the musician 'becomes' the music. Now man is constantly failing to atone for his 'original sin' of separation from *Brahman*. He is so completely identified with his body and mind that he spends all his energy in the attainment of the worldly goals and the pleasures of life. But the world is a system of causes and effects. So it is not surprising that he must reap as he sows. As long as a man remains identified with an ego-centered personality, he must remain implicated in the cycle of births and deaths in some or the other world. But it is possible to end this cycle. And it is each man's duty to choose a way of life, especially inwardly, so that he moves steadily towards salvation, the end of the chain of *karmic* influences. There are many ways to attain salvation for everyone irrespective of his present *karmic* condition. And it is God's promise to man that he will help him to attain salvation. Even in his worst *karmic* predicament man can break out of the spell of *karma* and attain *moksha* or salvation. Thus spoke Lord Krishna:

> Put aside all worldly demands of duties
> Just surrender to Me alone
> And I shall destroy your *karmic* sins
> And surely bless you with *moksha*.[5]

But "surrender to the Supreme Being" is not an easy matter. The accomplishment of surrender is constrained by one's *karmic* situation. One has to move within those constraints. But as we have seen, the individual is essentially free to improve his lot, to the extent that if he has the "courage to be", to be wholly authentic in his desire to return to his pure self, he can make a total break from all his *karmic* demerits here and now. The law of *karma* is a testimony of the scientific temper of our mystic seers and the Hindu philosopher-saints who have clearly shown that *karmic* determinants are not deterministic, but can be turned into one's favour in the pursuit of the ultimate goal of life. It exhorts us to action and tells us to assert our individuality. It warns us not to get lost with the faceless mass of humanity and not to get sucked into the meaningless battles of the materialistic world of today. The self-regulatory natural law of *karma* is in no way a threat, but rather a boon to the moral and spiritual freedom of man.

The twin doctrines of *karma* and rebirth go hand in hand. Indeed, as we have noted, the social status as well as the mental and moral potential of a person at his birth is determined by the *karma* of his previous life. "O Partha! those who have chosen the path of goodness for salvation they are never reborn in misery. They are born in enlightened and resourceful families or in the families of *yogins*. There in them arises the consciousness of previous life's attainments. And from these they move further towards salvation."[6] The doctrine of rebirth is a doctrine which has been held, in spite of their differences on the nature of the soul or the *atman*, by all the religions of the Indian origin. The earliest documented mention of the doctrine is in the *Brihadaranyaka Upanishad* composed around 1000 B.C. Many different types of consideration are brought forward to prove the truth of the doctrine. They range from the testimony of the *yogins* to the serious philosophical arrangements. Though all the theistic religions of the world believe in some form of survival after death, the belief in rebirth is peculiar to the Indian religion only. Even the youngest Indian religion, Sikhism, has retained the doctrine. Indeed, it is claimed that the belief is much older than Hinduism and was already held by the Jains and the *yoga* school of the pre-Aryan civilizations.

One way of assessing the value of the doctrine considered, as a probable hypothesis, could be to ask what the human situation would be like if it were not true. Morally and spiritually, what would be the human predicament if each soul had only one life. Well, we know that humans are born unequal, both in there mental as well as physical capacities. We know further that socially and in terms of their physical location, they are born unequal with respect to the opportunities for developing themselves and finding the fulfilment of life in general. And we also know that even those who are well placed in these respects can suffer a serious setback any time due to the contingencies of life, of accidents or illnesses or loss of wealth, etc. And above all, we know that even if everything goes fine with a person, one life is much too short to achieve moral or spiritual perfection. One has to be lucky to have heard of "the revealed message" in the first place. And what about all those souls who were born long before the revealed religions themselves were born? In such a situation on the hypothesis of 'one life' the world would surely appear to be much too senseless, even demonic, to have been created by a just God. Moreover, it is irrational to imagine that after death a soul is simply 'dormant' for a very very long time to rise only on the Day of Judgment to be punished or rewarded. The general objection against this belief is simply that a 'dormant' soul (or spirit) is just as good as no soul. A soul *qua* spirit must manifest occurrent appropriate activity. And the only way it can do this is through its implication in the order of existence. If, on the other hand, a soul at death is totally annihilated and, on the Day of Judgment, recreated by the power of God then again, logically, we could not talk of it being the same soul as the one stipulated. This is so because with the lack of continuity between the two souls, we could only speak of the 'recreated' soul to be exactly similar to the one it is supposed to be identical with. But similarity, however great, does not stand for identity. And God could not punish or reward a soul for being similar to the one whom he is supposed to be punishing or rewarding. The alternative would be to believe that a soul is simply a product of certain physical or chemical processes. But then that would be a materialist point of view and Hinduism (like any other religion) will hold no brief for it.

The twin doctrines of *karma* and rebirth change the picture completely. With the possibility of rebirth we have a meaningful world with unlimited opportunities for moral and spiritual progress. And this in turn, given the religious belief in the existence of a just and caring God, confirms the hypothesis of the doctrine of rebirth.

In consonance with my discussion as above Ninian Smart has written: "A . . . theological consideration in favour of rebirth . . . is the fact that belief in the doctrine chimes in with the idea that there are different grades of spiritual attainment. Thus the person of lowly stature now may gain a higher position in the next life . . . and so on. It is no doubt because of belief in rebirth that Indian views on conversion and in general on religious education are much more permissive than those which derive from the Semitic faiths."[7]

The Hindus also take the personal testimony of adept *yogins* seriously, who are able to recall their own and perceive other people's previous lives, with their supernatural powers acquired by the practice of *Hatha Yoga* (a branch of the *yoga* of consciousness which is supposed to awaken the *kundalini* or the psychic centres, located along the spinal chord of the human body). According to the stories of the Buddhist text, known as *Jatakas*, even the greatest sage-*yogin* Gautama the Buddha, is supposed to have recalled as many as five hundred and fifty of his earlier births, in various forms of living beings, during his meditations before attaining enlightenment. Thus, the wicked and the virtuous both pass through the cycle of rebirths. As the Hindus believe in numerous *lokas* or world-orders of different forms of consciousness, the humans may be reborn in other worlds as well, all according to the dictates of their *karma*. Some ascend to the heavens and some are cast into hell with subhuman species. And the rounds of births and deaths go on according to perfect justice enshrined in the law of *karma*. Thus, the doctrine of rebirth too like the doctrine of *karma* is sensitive to the moral function it is to serve in an essentially religious universe.

> "Where one's mind is attached the inner self
> goes thereto with *karma*, being attached
> to it alone. Obtaining the end of his
> action, whatever he does in this world
> he comes again
> from that world to this world of action."[8]

Apart from the above considerations, there is a more straightforward philosophical argument to prove rebirth. The belief in rebirth seems to follow from the premises containing the beliefs in *karma* and the soul. We have seen that the soul is indestructible and indivisible and it is implicated in the order of Nature. The soul, in its aspect of its involvement in the world, is constantly accumulating merits and demerits for its actions. And the law of *karma* is also eternally engaging. As long as the soul is implicated in the psycho-physical state of the implicated soul, it is not the end of the soul's involvement with the elements. Given these premises, it seems to follow (logically) that the soul will be impelled to carry on with its involvement with a post-mortem psycho-physical entity as directed by the requirements of the law of *karma*. In other words, the soul has no option but to be reborn. This process must go on until it receives the final issuing of eternal freedom from the round of rebirths. Transmigration of souls works on the secular principle of cause and effect without any divine interference. Though, for the theist, the law of cause and effect itself is the manifestation of the divine will. The Hindu God has installed a system of justice, which works eternally on its own accord. He does not have to wait for some Day of Judgment when all the cases will be dealt with once for ever. The above argument, though not explicitly stated, is implied in the *Gita:*

> As a man discards worn-out clothes
> And puts on others that are new,
> The embodied soul casts off bodies old
> Receiving others anew.[9]

And the doctrine is fully endorsed in the *Katha Upanishad* much before the *Gita:*

> The wise one is not born, nor does he die
> He has not come from anywhere,
> Nor has become anyone.
> Unborn, unchanging, eternal, original,
> He (the soul) is not slain in the slaying of the body.[10]

As far as the mechanism of rebirth is concerned, it is more of a problem for philosophy. For the present context, it will suffice us to note that first in Hinduism the soul or the *atman*, being an immaterial substance which is essentially non-spatial, is considered to be all-pervasive, i.e., not bound by its location in the body which it informs at the given time and place. Next, this makes it possible to accept its another doctrine, that of "causation at the distance". Now the rebirth is explained as the operation of the moral forces, of an all-pervasive soul, left over from its earlier embodiment. But the more widely held belief is that the soul, as considered implicated in the order of nature, the *Jivatma* (or simply the *jiva*), at the time of the physical death, moves out of the dead body but still embodied in a subtle body or *sukchma sarira*. It is the subtle body that is the carrier of the merits and the demerits of *karma* which will determine the status of the soul in the next birth. Even the distinctness of the soul in relation to Nature is determined by the character of the subtle body, since the souls *qua* the inner self of individuals have essentially the same nature. And in the ultimate analysis, souls are considered to be the inalienable 'parts' of the universal soul. The word 'part' should not be taken literally. The universal soul like the individual souls are, as we have seen, indivisible and indestructible. The individual souls are parts of the soul only when considered from the empirical standpoint, in so far as, from that point of view, souls are identified by reference to individual egos, which in turn are identified by reference to the psycho-physical entity which souls inform. It is something like the mystery of the Trinity. The individual souls are numerous, yet by virtue of having the same essence as the universal self, they are, ontologically, one with the universal soul. All the same, it must be admitted that the mechanism of rebirth is somewhat esoteric. But then we cannot understand the occult without having the relevant kind of experiences. Hinduism recommends *yoga* to enable you to have those experiences.

If the idea of the subtle body, as the carrier of the 'tendencies' determining the potential personality at rebirth, sounds peculiar the following considerations may help the reader to understand. Firstly, as we have noted, the Hindu psychology does not admit a sharp ontological distinction between the mental and the physical. Secondly, in our times there is a very good analogy available as a model, from the case of the transfer of thought from one brain to another through the 'subtle body' of radio waves. Similarly, the 'mental' does not literally need the brain for its transport. As long as some subtle energy of the brain is released at death, it can be imagined to carry the mental elements necessary for actualizing a rebirth of a particular soul. The Hindus believe that this mechanism of soul-transfer at rebirth has been experienced by the adept *yogins* in their extra-sensory perceptions.

A more scientifically viable analogy will be this. Imagine a super scientist who is able to 'lift' all the information in the brain cells of *A* and transfer it systematically to the previously 'cleaned' brain cells of *B*. *B* will now speak with the identity of *A*. In this experiment the lifting in question is equivalent to the death of *A* and the transfer to the brain of *B* is equivalent to the rebirth of *A* in the body of *B*. If the mechanism of 'subtle body' is the nature's way of lifting and transfer at a natural death and birth, then there seems no, in principle, difficulty in accepting the doctrine of rebirth.

At all times, however, it remains true that rebirth is controlled by the law of *karma*, both in its psychological and moral aspects. In both these aspects *karma* derives its operational potential from the nature of actions performed during a given life. For a 'good' rebirth (i.e., a rebirth in which the individual is born endowed with such psychological and moral attributes which are conducive to his further spiritual growth towards the final liberation), one must choose to live an active life with a sense of responsibility and spiritual detachment. First, as the *Gita* rightly observes that even one's simple physical existence cannot be preserved without appropriate action. Moreover, action is not only necessary but also inevitable.

> For no one ever for a moment can
> Remain without action.
> Helplessly all are impelled to act
> From the impulses born of nature."[11]

So, next, given the inevitability of acting, how should one act to attain a good rebirth?

> The action performed in inattention
> Without regard to loss and injury,

> Without consideration of one's human capacity,
> Is said to be of the nature of 'inaction'.[12]

And to gain moral merit for a good rebirth the *Gita* recommends:

> Except work done in the spirit of sacrifice
> This world is in bondage,
> The works tie you to the worldly gains,
> So O Kaunteya! act always impartially.
> Without the motive of personal gain.[13]

And again,

> Perform always your duties
> Without attachment to the gains from actions,
> For living thus in non-attachment
> Man attains the highest spiritual status.[14]

REFERENCES

1. *Manusmriti*, 9, 300.
2. *Gita*, 9, 21.
3. *Chandogya Upanishad*, 6, 2, 3.
4. IV, 4.5.
5. *Gita*, 18, 66.
6. *Ibid.*, 6, 40, 43.
7. "Doctrine and Argument" in *Indian Philosophy*, London, 1964, p. 163.
8. *Brihadaranyaka Upanishad*, IV, 4, 6.
9. *Gita*, 2, 22.
10. II, 18.
11. 3, 5.
12. *Gita*, 18, 25.
13. 3, 9.
14. 3, 19.

5

THE INCARNATION OF GOD
(Avatar)

O Parth! behold Me now
In my hundreds and thousands of Forms
In numerous constitutions and divinities
In numerous colours, and shapes.[1]

It is somewhat surprising that several theistic religions of the world do not believe in the doctrine of incarnation of God. They find it illogical and even repugnant to the religious sensibility of man. As against this view, Hinduism, the first religion to propose the doctrine, upholds that incarnation is not only consistent with other Hindu beliefs, it is in fact required by any consistent faith which believes in the existence of personal God. Incarnation is man's ultimate hope towards certainty in the possibility of his own salvation. It is his innocent desire as God's creature that he should hear God's words from Himself. In his human situation, when man has reached a certain stage of maturity in his biological and mental evolution, when he realizes that he has been thrown in this vast unknown, in the midst of uncertainties and ignorance, with his limited powers of understanding, is it not natural for his religious instincts to hope that the truth would one day manifest on the earth and communicate itself to man? And is it not natural for him to believe that this would happen, then and again, whenever he is thrown into scepticism due to his own advancement in material knowledge? And should he not even pray that incarnation should happen then and always when man has fallen so low in the temptations of the flesh that he has grown so weak in his will that he is left with no hope to save himself on his own? Indeed he should. As the sages of the Hindus prayed:

> Lead me to *Brahman*
> from what is NOT.
> Lead me to light
> From darkness,
> Lead me to Everlasting Life,
> From the mortal death.[2]

And now look at the human situation from the point of view of God, who is the Lord, the ruler of all that is born and unborn. Moreover, God is not just the 'ruler', distanced and external as it were to all beings. He is the actual creator of all beings as Krishna speaks in the *Gita:*

> O Kaunteya! all beings,
> At the end of a world-eon,
> Return to my manifest Nature.
> And at the beginning of a new
> World-eon I recreate them all.[3]

Thus, Nature is only a manifestation of divine attributes, in which God, like the father, implants the seed of life. All beings are dependent upon Nature, but Nature itself is dependent upon God. It is God who activates Nature in the first place. It is God who sustains its functions and then at the end of the world-cycle withdraws it into Himself. The entire cycle of the universe's creation, maintenance and dissolution depends completely on the power of God. When such God looks upon his creatures, who are in a hopeless situation, disillusioned and surrounded with evil, it is natural for Him to be moved by His own compassionate and caring nature to do something to help the human beings. But He has to move within certain constraints emanating from His own will. We know that in Hinduism the universe is governed by the law of *karma*. Hinduism does not believe in miraculous interventions in human history, out of tune with the law of *karma*. God has endowed man with free will and given him all the potentialities to help him to seek out the Lord and his personal salvation. It is man's own sowing that he now reaps a hopeless situation. But, in principle, man is always capable of getting out of it and reorganizing his life in such a way so that he begins to move again towards his ultimate goal of salvation within a basically righteous world-order. So within these constraints what is the most rational way for a compassionate God to help man out of his terrible predicament?

I think the answer is clear. God has somehow to recreate the righteous order of life. He has to bring to man that truth which will free him from his own weakness of the will. He has to awaken man's mind and heart to realize his potentialities so that his faith in himself returns. He has to give man the certainty, not through absolute forgiveness, but through this promise that through his own efforts man would be saved and find the abode of the Eternal. How can God achieve all this? The answer is obvious. God has to incarnate amidst human beings. And this is what Krishna declares:

> I am never born, never destroyed,
> I am the Lord of all beings,
> And with my own manifest nature
> By my own will, I incarnate in the world.[4]

I think it is obvious that the Eternal has to enter the temporal as a human being. And through his own example, operating within the framework of the Law, He has to organize the destruction of the evil and reveal the truth convincingly to enable man to reorganize his life within the order of goodness. And this is the *raision d'etre* of incarnation. Incarnation is a part of the divine plan for the world. He comes into the world as often as He feels the need for it. And He comes in the world in non-human forms as well if need be so. And He incarnates with a varying number of *kalas*, i.e., 'specialized powers' according to the need of the situation. Occasionally, He makes a 'full' incarnation. By that is meant that He comes in the world in a human form through a miraculous, though in all appearance a normal human, birth to a woman, possessing all the sixteen *kalas* and displays a full participation in the human life of a civilization He has chosen through enacting the major role He has chosen to play. The number 'sixteen' for all the *kalas* does not mean that these are all the attributes that God possesses. What it means is that these are all the attributes or specialized powers which are relevant to human life and which may be invoked by the Incarnate-God in acting out His role as a human being. The use of these powers are, therefore, not meant to be treated as miracles, but only as somewhat superhuman exercises.

In the history of incarnations, Lord Rama and Lord Krishna are believed to be full incarnations. Rama and Krishna are not proved to be 'historical', like Buddha or Christ, in the modern sense of the word 'history'. But given the fact that in the distant past history was preserved either through the oral traditions or in writing, in the religious traditions, Hindus have sufficient reason to believe in their historicity (It may also be noted that in the recent years certain excavations in the State of Haryana, where the famous battle of Kurukshetra, depicted in the *Gita*, was fought, have provided some evidence to the modern historians, for the historicity of Lord Krishna). Before Rama and Krishna, there are supposed to be several other incarnations to accomplish a particular end which was not possible for the humans to achieve. These incarnations are in various different life forms depending upon the needs of the situation. Of these, the most famous one is that of *Narasingha*, which literally means 'Man-Lion'. *Narasingha* was half-human (in the lower half of the body) and lion in the upper half of the body. And he had come to destroy a devil-incarnate who ruled the earth and proclaimed himself to be God. He would torture those who would not surrender to him and accept him as the Supreme Being. Among the tortured happened to be his own son, Prahalada who was a profound devotee of God and worshipped Him alone. In his earlier life the devil had worshipped Lord Shiva and obtained a boon from him that he will not be killed either by a man or a beast, either on the earth or in the air. Nor would he be killed by any weapon of man or of the gods. But the boon had obviously gone to his head. The form of '*Narasingha*' was chosen since the boon had to be respected. The devil was killed by *Narasingha* at the end of the day before the night fell placed in his own lap, with his own lion-paws. In this way all the terms of the boon were unviolated and the devil was destroyed and the devil's son was saved to rule the earth with due respect for the Supreme Being.

The main reason for God's full incarnation as a human being is declared in the *Gita* by Krishna himself:

> "O Bharata! Whenever
> Religion has declined to its lowest
> And evil is flourishing
> Then, ever and again I incarnate.
> To save the sages
> And destroy the wicked
> To reestablish the Order of Goodness
> I incarnate from *Yuga* to *Yuga*".[5]

(In popular Hindu belief, one world-cycle is constituted of four *yugas* or eons. And each cycle consists of twelve million human years).

In the philosophical parlance God's incarnation is presented as a paradox. How can the Eternal enter into the temporal, asks Kierkegaard (Soren Kierkegaard, *Concluding Unscientific Postscript*, trs. D. Swanson and W. Lowrie, Princeton, 1941, p. 206)? How can He give man the truth when man is not capable of receiving it? How will man recognize the truth when it comes to him? Puzzled with such questions Kierkegaard was led to declare that faith in the incarnation of God is a paradox.

It seems to me, however, that this puzzle involves a misreading of the doctrine. The doctrine of incarnation does not require that the Eternal actually becomes the temporal. Or, that the omnipotent being has somehow shrunk into a causally dependent particular in the body of a human being. In the Hindu belief what it means is, as we have seen, that an actual human person is informed by the power of God to live a certain kind of life chosen by the will of God. The life of Krishna lived with all his potentialities, for example, was not determined by his prior *karma*. Krishna has no antecedent *karmic* influences. His life is a pure 'beginning' designed to fulfil a certain purpose. While living Krishna does not accumulate any *karma* either.

> The works I perform
> Do not implicate Me (into *Karma*)
> Nor do I carry any desire
> For personal fulfilment from works.[6]

The theory of incarnation has to cross two gaps. The first is the one already discussed in the chapter on God. It is the gap between the absolutist concept of God and the determinate concept of God as a personal being endowed with virtues relevant to human existence, as the embodiment of Truth, Goodness and Beauty. Hinduism, as we have seen, fills this gap by declaring that the eternal-Absolute manifests itself, quite spontaneously as the Supreme Being the personal God. If the eternal-Absolute did not manifest as the Primary person (*Paramatma*) it would be an uncreative absolute it would be absolutely inert. Then there would have been no creation to follow. But the Hindu believes that the universe (including all living beings) is a product of God's creativity. And since the universe is a meaningful causally interdependent and therefore intelligible 'whole', it must be initially an act of a creative intelligence, a unitary centre of primordial consciousness, which can be represented as 'the source of all manifest energy'. It must be the personal God postulated in all the advanced religions of the world which the Hindu sees as the embodiment of *Satyam, Shivam, Sundaram*, or Truth, Goodness and Beauty.

The second gap is most baffling, as reflected in Kierkegaard's despair at the thought of incarnation as presented in Christianity and his perception of it as a paradox. As he could not solve the puzzle, he declared that this is where the notion of faith gets a foothold in religion. A paradox is a proper object of faith. But surely, there is a difference between 'blind' faith and faith as a reasonable belief. The latter has to be based in a sound rational intuition which itself must arise from the background of a coherent view of reality. The Hindu belief in incarnation is as sound and reasonable as any non-empirical belief can ever be.

Firstly, the eternal as a personal god has been made intelligible, as we have seen, by being portrayed in the bodily form appropriate to the ascription of a personality to God. Then the intelligibility of the idea of incarnation as the 'spiritual animation' of a human body with the attributes relevant to human life and appropriate to God Himself is only a step away. There is no difficulty in imagining that a personal god as conceived by the Hindus can without abandoning his heavenly abode, actually energize the body of a human child in such a way so that he deserves the title of God-Incarnate.

However, it would be retorted that the puzzle is still not completely solved. The Hindu god is still the eternal reality; how can the eternal have anything to do with temporal? The answer lies in distinguishing between the two senses of 'eternal'. In one sense 'eternal' means 'timeless' or 'non-temporal', but in another sense it means 'everlasting'. The former adopts a transcendental perspective upon Reality. The latter sense exemplifies the empirical standpoint and signifies the discursive truth that God is everlasting through 'all conceivable time'. And since time is psychologically irremovable from empirically structured consciousness, ever-lastingness seems to be just as good as non-temporality. So the paradox of the eternal entering into the temporal is not ontological; it is simply conceptual and arises out of a shift of perspective upon the reality of God.

So, Krishna is not subject to the law of rebirth on account of the accumulation of merits and demerits of *karma*. Krishna's presence in the world is accounted for only by God's will, *ab initio*, to incarnate to help the ailing humanity. This he does first by clearing the ground from the prevailing evils and then by revealing the eternal Truth governing the world including human existence. When Krishna reveals his cosmic powers in the famous vision of the *Gita* to Arjuna, he established both, the truth of God's incarnation as well as the truth of *Dharma*, i.e., the order of righteous living. Further, he reveals the truth of all the central doctrines of the Hindu faith in the actual experience of Arjuna. And Krishna revealing his true nature as God speaks:

> The *devas* and the *maharishis*
> Do not know the source of My existence
> Because it is Me only.
> Who is the cause of their origin
>
> Among the mortals
> Who know Me as the Supreme Master
> And know Me as unborn and eternal
> They are freed from all sins.
>
> I am the Source of
> The different states in living beings;
> The intellect, knowledge, enlightenment
> Forgiveness, truth and sense perceptions,
> Peace, pleasure and pain, birth and death,
> Fear and fearlessness, non-violence, impartiality,
> Contendedness, austerity, charity, fame and notoriety.[7]

And revealing himself thus as the supreme monotheistic truth, Krishna gives Arjuna the vision of his cosmic body. 'Shining greater than thousands of suns put together, without beginning, without end, pervading the entire universe'. And finding it too overwhelming Arjuna cries out:

> Having seen your cosmic body,
> Unperceived by man before,
> I am awed and trembling,
> Shaken by fear and dread.
> So, O Lord! O universal Person!
> Be pleased and return to your earthly form.[8]

The total significance of this episode for the doctrine of *avatar* is clear enough. Firstly, the Lord had shown his cosmic reality on Arjuna's own request. It is not that Arjuna was not convinced of the truth of Krishna's discourse on his cosmic nature. But Arjuna wants to go beyond the mere intellectual conviction to an experiential understanding of it, wondering if it were 'at all possible' for a flesh-and-blood human being to experience God in this very life. By heeding to Arjuna's request Krishna establishes for good that it is possible with the grace of God and that God would listen to man's prayer if it were sincere. Such experiential conviction would not have been generated in Arjuna if the vision had come 'out of the blue', as it were, or if he was informed by some 'voice' or 'angel'. Its authenticity is fully established only against the background of the belief in Krishna's *avatara*. More generally, the doctrine of incarnation is expedient in another way. It enables us to integrate the two, apparently opposing, aspects of 'transcendence' and 'immanence' in the actual nature of God, for it is easier to move from the concrete to the abstract. And through Arjuna's experience of the cosmic body of the incarnate-God, we can immediately understand both God's immanence and His transcendence.

Avatara, therefore, underscores the immense possibilities of man's relationship with God. It displays man's own ultimate potentialities for salvation and returns his 'faith in God'. This would not be possible if man simply heard a mysterious voice or saw something extraordinary to be believed as a miracle performed by God. Without a proper background, there would be no rationale to hold such events to be exemplifying the will of God. The momentous event of *avatara*, therefore, provides the required background:

> I am the goal, the sustainer of the universe
> The supreme Lord, the witness and the Abode
> The refuge, friend, source, destroyer and support
> The Treasure and the eternal cause.[9]

To conclude, I have suggested that faith in the incarnation of God is not a paradox. The Hindu doctrine of *avatara* believes that there can be different degrees of manifestation of the divine presence in the world. This can occur in different intelligent life-forms at different times in different historical contexts (Thus, in principle, a Hindu should have no problem with the Christian belief in the status of Christ). Next, though a given *avatara* has a specific end to achieve, namely, the destruction of a specific evil, its long term goal is to reestablish the righteous order of existence. And its most general purpose is to reveal the truth, which includes not only the existence of a personal God but also the truth of other central doctrines of Hinduism. Moreover, it is achieved in a most convincing manner through inter-personal relationship between the Incarnate-person and other human persons participating in the life lived out by the Incarnation. It also provides proof of God's concern for the world and his creatures. And it shows us the way to look up to God to seek his grace for our personal salvation into *moksha*.

REFERENCES

1. *Gita*, 11, 5.
2. *Brihadaranyaka Upanishad*, 11, 5.
3. *Gita*, 9, 7.
4. *Ibid.*, 4, 6.
5. *Ibid.*, 4, 7-8.
6. *Ibid.*, 4, 14.
7. *Ibid.*, 10, 2-5.
8. *Ibid.*, 11, 45.
9. *Ibid.*, 9, 18.

6

MOKSHA
(Liberation or Spiritual Freedom)

> Free us from the yoke of
> The sins of our fathers and
> Those that we ourselves have committed.
> Set free your servant as a
> Thief is forgiven for his crime
> Or as a calf is from its post.[1]

Hinduism is the earliest religion of mankind, which has characterized the religious end of life, *moksha* in terms of spiritual freedom. From its popular rendition as 'freedom from rebirth', *moksha* has developed into a deep philosophical understanding of freedom in its existential context. It is a freedom while one is still alive—a freedom from having to be one's fears and sorrows. It is a freedom from the mistaken consciousness of one's identity with the psycho-physical reality of embodiment, and consequently, a freedom from rebirth. In religious terms it amounts to personal salvation and a condition in which the human soul has achieved a release from the implicate order of existence, the *sansara*. The concept of *moksha* has two sides to it, naturally, since *moksha* is both a 'freedom-from' and a 'freedom-into'. Of these, the latter has received three major interpretations. But the aspect of 'freedom-from' is common to all the Hindu philosophical systems.

It will be seen that in Hinduism 'spiritual freedom' represents a wholly different phenomenon than that suggested by 'salvation' in the religions of the Semitic tradition. This is so primarily because to the Hindu mind the quest of salvation arises from the existential human predicament rather than from the background of beliefs taken to be 'revealed truths' coming from God in Heaven. The Hindu *moksha* requires a disciplined quest of the eternal truth. First and foremost, it is a quest into the 'inner' reality of one's own being. The 'self' is at the centre of man's personal existence. A sincere quest of truth, therefore, must involve self-knowing. And the journey into the self must bring about a radical transformation of the seeker—a change, which renews the entire human being including his sentiments and his total attitude towards life.

Hinduism perceives the human situation as that of 'spiritual bondage'. Though man appears, at the surface, to be free to feel, think and act, in ways, as he desires, he fails to realize that his desires themselves are the factor of bondage. Through his own attachment to pleasures and possessions, through his own desire for personal fulfilment, man is gradually enslaved by his own passions. This lands him into great sorrow. For life, being what it is, he is frequently frustrated in his aims.

> In the contemplation of pleasures
> One develops attachment in them
> From attachment one is led to indulge in desires
> From (frustration of) desires one experiences anger
> From anger arises mental bewitchment
> From bewitchment memory defaults
> And memory defaulting discriminating intelligence is lost
> And losing intelligence one is as good as dead.[2]

This deep psychology of the motivational structure behind every day life explains beautifully how bondage is set in. The bondage consists in the 'impelling and conditioning character of emotions'. In the natural course of events one is led to live a life of chain reactions. One is caught up in the network of self-seeking activities without any appreciation of their overall significance for the meaning and purpose of life as a whole.

Moreover, certain universal features of life, such as the loss of the loved ones, disease, old age and death, inevitably bring enormous 'fears' to the human heart and consequently tremendous sorrows to mankind. In face of these evils embedded in the human situation, therefore, a sensitive man is naturally led to seek inner spiritual freedom in life—a freedom or *mukti* which can end his fears and pains of sufferings and sorrows once for all.

Spiritual freedom is the ultimate goal of human life. The doctrine of *moksha* constitutes the very distinctive core of Hinduism. It makes the most original and fundamental contribution to man's religious quest of the meaning of life. *Moksha*, in one form or the other, is retained in all the religions of Indian origin, including Buddhism, which has branched off from Hinduism. In the Hindu philosophy, though the concept has received several very illuminating interpretations, there is an amazing seamless continuity of the central theme. Given the long sweep of the history of Hinduism, this is only to be expected. But this has only enriched our understanding of the central tenets of the doctrine. Let us see how the Hindu scriptures elucidate the meaning of '*moksha*'.

In order to appreciate the full spiritual significance of *moksha* we will have to study it in three different perspectives upon it. These are 'existential', 'metaphysical' and 'transcendental'. It will be seen, however, that this approach, far from being fragmentary, yields an integrated total understanding of the doctrine. In the existential perspective, we will explore the character of the actual life of a person who has received the blessing of *moksha* before his temporal death in this world. We will explore the nature of the transformation in his physical and mental relationship with the world and his own experience of life, as we commonly know it. In the metaphysical perspective, we will assess mainly the meaning of *moksha* in relation to the possibility of rebirth or the possibility of his continuing personal existence on a higher plane of the cosmic order. And, in the transcendental perspective, we will be concerned with the spiritual status of the soul of a *moksha*-realized man in relation to God or the Absolute.

Further, since Hinduism is rooted in the deep reflective traditions of the *Vedas*, the sages have sought freedom from the existential paradoxes of life, which are universal in human experience. First, at the heart of the human-reality there exists the paradox of 'being and becoming'. It arises because, on the one hand, the human being perceives himself as a unitary centre of conscious to which all his experiences are assigned. In this perception he represents himself as a soul—a permanent, indivisible, spiritual entity. On the other hand, in introspection, he does not see the soul, or any other attribute, which will identify him uniquely. Rather, he tends to identify himself with moment to moment contents of his personal consciousness. That is, he identifies himself not with something permanent, but a perpetual flux of mental events—he *can be* something only by moment to moment becoming. This paradox of self-identification is rooted in a more fundamental 'duality' of self and non-self. Put simply, it is like this. Whatever the self looks at and perceives as an object—either in the world or in his own mind—is obviously not the subject-self. The true seer always escapes himself. Thus, everything perceived is 'outside' the seer. As we have seen, the contents of self-consciousness constitute only the 'empirical self', not the *atman*. The Hindu concept of '*moksha*' claims to end this conflict-ridden paradoxical existence. The *moksha*-realized man attains a higher consciousness which transcends the structures of the experience of the subject-object dualism altogether. In essence, *moksha* consists in ending the existential separation between the human spirit and the divine reality. It is generally believed by Hindu thinkers that in the state of spiritual freedom the individual ego is either completely submerged in the universal self, or, if freedom is attained while one is still alive, the ego is marginalized to a mere functional level of operation necessary for day-to-day physical existence. Unfortunately, the ego is exhalted to the level of the true self, the *atman*. And the satisfaction of the ego becomes the all-important aim in life. We fall in bondage to the desires arising from the egoistic-self and forget man's natural desire for true happiness.

The Existential Character of Freedom

At the existential level the fulfilment of *moksha* is termed '*jivanmukti*' or living-release. A *jivanmukta* is free from the illusion of his true identity as the empirical self because he is constantly aware of the *atman* which is eternally free. His choices in the temporal world flow from his background awareness of this continuing transcendence. That is, he is simultaneously aware both of his embodied being as well as his spiritual being. Though his ego is still implicated in the temporal order of the objective world, its movements are constantly guided and restrained by the higher truth.

Such a person is no longer self-indulgent. He is fully conscious of the futility of chasing personal pleasures. He sees that the 'I' is not the actual doer of his actions. The I-consciousness wrongly identifies itself as the 'owner' of all its experiences. It is an illusion to think that the 'I' is the primary source of those experiences. "The enlightened saint sees that there is no 'doer' apart from the *gunas*. . . ."[3] (*Gunas* are three in number. They are the foundational qualities or entities of Nature, which have partly physical and partly psychological characteristics. It is from the interaction of these qualities or strand-substances that all other determinate things come into beings. The strand-substances are called *satvik, rajsik* and *tamsik*. The first represents lucidity and higher mental functions. The second represents volatility and is a carrier of energy. The third represents dullness and sluggishness and constitutes the mass and the density of material objects. The experiences arise through the interactive processes between the body and the mind, and the 'I', which is an independent category in the manifest Nature, mingles with all the experiences arising in separate psycho-physical entities. The *Gita* states clearly that the ego, together with the mind and the intellect, and the five categories of the material nature—Earth, Water, Fire, Air and Space—are separate manifestations of the divine nature.[4] The *Gita* also states that all works are performed by the three *Gunas* alone, but the egoistic man believes that "I am the doer".[5]

Living without the 'I', in the sense of its role consigned simply to functional relationships, must be an extraordinary experience. Firstly, it must be an experience of 'timelessness' considered in its subjective qualification. Let us call it "psychological time" (a term used by J. Krishnamurti) as distinct from the more familiar 'chronological time'. The latter is time measured by the watch. It is 'objective' and shared by all. History is a record of this time. And one has to keep an eye on this time in order to move around in the world. But the psychological time is created by the memories of the past and the hopes and fears of the future. It is a personal expanse of consciousness—a space between a personal past and a projected personal future. In the objective world there is no past as such, obviously, or else it would be existing in the 'now'. Nor is there a future as such or else it would not be something yet to be. In reality, all existence is in the "now". But we believe in a 'real' future in which our desires will be fulfilled. Our hopes, ambitions and despair are all located in the psychological time. It is the time in which we execute our plans to 'attain' and to 'become' this or that. Our personal ambitions for wealth, power and recognition, and lamentations over the irretrievable losses, in fact, constitute the psychological time. It is clear, then, that the death of the 'I' will bring freedom from the psychological past and future and, therefore, freedom from the burden of hopes and ambitions and the consequent fears of failure. The *jivanmukta* is not impelled to act by the desires of 'becoming' or personal success. In fact, 'desire (apart from those concerned with the necessities of survival) is considered inherently an exemplar of un-freedom. We can see the truth of this if we attend to the fact that desire is always exercising some influence on the will. Depending on the strength of one's desire the will is coerced into struggling for its fulfilment. In the very arousal of a desire there is a feeling of being compelled to move in a particular direction. Desire is never pure spontaneity. It arises from the conditioned background of attachment and burdens one with its demands. Each fulfilment further strengthens the desire and the struggle continues. What is even more remarkable is that even a failure in fulfilment further strengthens the desire, which, in face of subsequent failures, has to be suppressed. A mind complicated in this way cannot experience the joy and the spontaneity of freedom.

So the experience of timelessness in this sense must be an experience of inner spiritual peace and happiness. As the *Gita* maintains:

> Free from attachment and envy
> One who is in control of his senses
> One whose mind works under his own direction.
> He, though engaging in the works of the senses,
> Receives the blessing of a joyous consciousness.[6]

Living without the psychological 'I' is also a freedom from the sense of pride. Pride brings a whole chain of mental states resulting in suffering. The pride is inflated with every success of the 'me'. And it bestows a sense of importance—a vanity and further egoism. This feeling of the inflated 'me' inevitably results in conflict and the struggle to end it. But the struggle is unending, since one has to maintain one's importance all along. The struggle is always accompanied with pain, even though one may experience occasional flashes of pleasure at some or the other success.

With the 'I' marginalized to its functional role, the *jivanmukta* lives his life without any sense of pride on success and shame at failure. The greatest bondage of man is his deep inward fear of the temporal world. The world is 'external' to the 'I' which gives a permanent sense of separation from being. A duality is set in and there is a vast uncertainty about one's relationship with the world. Being frightened of this uncertainty we are easily coerced into conformity, obedience and imitation. We are afraid of all sorts of things, disease, old age, death, poverty, loneliness, public opinion, not being able to accomplish anything spiritually, etc. etc. And being frightened we live our lives under pressure—to find some emotional security and some passing pleasures here and there. But fear is a constant reminder of one's insufficiency and incapability. This adds sorrow to the frightened mind. The *jivanmukta* is free from this fear and sorrow, for he has gained the experiential knowledge of the great *upanishadic* truth 'Thou art That' implying that You are the world. The *jivanmukta*, living without the 'I', is living in love—love that is not possessive, that 'seeketh not its own'. When a man is free from the self-seeking desires then he lives his life for the 'love of life'. In the absence of the 'I' in selflessness, love is not the desire to possess, or to be possessed by, the object one loves. 'Possession' either way, involves a denial of freedom. Nor is 'attachment' an expression of love. In attachment the lover demands submission from the loved one. He is anxious to retain control over her. And this results in the loss of loyalty by the loved one. Thus fear, anxiety and violence are natural cognates of attachment. But this is quite the opposite of what we expect of love. Love is the primordial spiritual abode of the human spirit. Love ends conflicts, brings peace to the lover. It brings a sense of completeness and a sense of freedom from the burden of possession.

Both 'possession' and 'attachment' signify self-centered activity. If love is neither of these, then 'love of life' is a state of sensitivity and dynamism, signifying living in freedom of self-abandonment. In love one lives like an artist of life—creatively. By 'living creatively' I do not mean necessarily engaged in one of the arts. Living creatively is living in the moment to moment newness of life. Creativity lends a freshness to the very perception of life and a spontaneity to all one's responses in life. Spontaneity is freedom from the manipulative, self-indulgent 'becoming'. Love of life is inspired and replenished by the love of God. The *jivanmukta*, being in full contact with the hidden reality of *Brahman*, relates to all beings with the feeling that they all existed in his own being. He perceives God in everything and all things in God. Thus Krishna maintains:

> Seeing everyone in his own being
> And himself in every being,
> The *jivanmukta yogin* gives
> Impartial attention to all beings.
> He who feels my presence everywhere

Seeing everything in Me
I never lose sight of him
And he does never lose Me.[7]

The Metaphysical Character of Freedom

Now, in its metaphysical accretions '*moksha*' straightforwardly signifies 'freedom from the round of rebirth'. Since, as we have seen rebirth is a central doctrine in Hinduism, this aspect of freedom is most significant. It underlines the fact that *moksha* is not a passing temporary affair, it is everlasting. It is the first and the last spiritual freedom of the soul which, as we have seen, is implicated in a (beginning less) involvement with Nature and the consequent successive births and deaths and, given the doctrine of *karma*, *moksha* in the sense of freedom from rebirth amounts to a total ending of the accumulation of merits and demerits through the *karmic* requirements of works in life on earth.

It is important to realize that in freedom from rebirth, the free soul is not going to be born even in the heavenly abodes. In the Hindu belief heavens and hells are included in the world-order (the *sansara*). And even the most pious and virtuous soul, who has not yet attained *moksha* having lived his life on earth, is reborn in heavenly abodes. And having enjoyed the rewards of his virtuous life in heaven exhausting the merits earned, he is returned back to the earth. The *Gita* declares:

The doers of works prescribed in the three *Vedas*
Having consumed their purifying *Somrasa* (Nectar of life),
Worshipping Me, ask for Heaven.
They reach the abode of gods and enjoy life there.
But having consumed the pleasures of the vast Heaven
Exhausting their merits, they return to the world of death.
Thus the doers of the three duties, desiring the fruits
of their works, remain entangled in the cycle of rebirth.[8]

In freedom from rebirth the soul is liberated beyond the heavens and ali the cycles of existence. This freedom is available not only to those who have attained living-release or *jivanmukti*. It is available to all the seers and saints of true faith in God—to all those who have lived, until their death, a truly religious life devoted to God. So Krishna says:

> O Arjuna! those who know in essence
> The mystery of my Incarnation, works and
> My divinity, they after leaving their bodies at death
> Never receive rebirth, rather they receive Me.[9]

Entering into the final state of *moksha*, however, may be postponed for a while by the *jivanmukta* on his own free will. This happens when the *jivanmukta* decides to continue his personal existence on a higher plane of consciousness after his death on the earth. He may do so in order to keep guiding his followers and others on earth who are seriously carrying on with the quest of *moksha*. And as soon as he desires to enter *moksha* eternally, he is able to do that. We can now move on to the discussion of the transcendental meaning of *moksha*.

The Transcendental Character of Freedom

In the transcendental aspect of freedom we are mainly concerned with two themes. One is about the nature of the internal fulfilment of the liberated soul in the state of eternity, and the other is about the ontological status of the liberated soul *vis-a-vis* both the *Sagun-Brahman*, i.e., the personal God, and the *Nirguna-Brahman* i.e., the suprapersonal divine Reality. Of these, the second theme, having fallen in the hands of philosophers, has been developed in various view-points. But the first theme has a single religious meaning. Let me elucidate the second theme first.

There are three main schools of thought; though they all claim that their view-points are reflected in the *Vedas*, they vary greatly in substance. These are known as *Advaita* (non-dualism), *Vishisthadvaita* (qualified non-dualism) and *Dvaita* (Dualism) together comprising the *Vedanta* school of Hindu religious philosophy. These view-points are commentaries on the same basic scripture called *Brahmasutra* or *Vedantasutra* which itself is a summation of the doctrines of the *Upanishads* and which was composed by Badarayana around the third century B.C.[10]

From the point of view of religious practice, the most revered exponent of the *Advaita* view-point is Shankara. We have already alluded to Shankara's distinction between *Nirguna Brahman* and *Sagun Brahman*. Shankara, who lived in the eighth century A.D., was a great campaigner for Hinduism. He is known to have great debates with Buddhists and almost eliminated their hold on the Hindu mind. He established four *dhamas* or holy shrines which are still the major places of pilgrimage for all Hindus. The sites, he selected for the *dhamas*, are situated in the four extreme geographical directions of the country—Rameswaram in the South, Puri in the East, Kedarnath in the North and Dwarka in the West—thus reaffirming the religious and the cultural unity of India.

Shankara's philosophy is known as 'non-dualism'. In this he is not denying that until *moksha* the individual's experience is bound up with the world of plurality. His non-dualism is about the post-*moksha* experience of the ultimate reality. He maintains that a liberated soul loses all consciousness of his individuality or his separateness from the world. The soul and the world merge into the undifferentiated *Brahman*. The liberated soul has no separate status. He is like the wave which 'belongs to the ocean and not the ocean to the wave (Radhakrishnan, *op. cit.*, p. 38). In this sense the liberated soul becomes *Brahman*. In the state of *moksha* the individual is nothing but *Brahman* which has but one uniform nature.[11] And the internal fulfilment of the liberated soul is characterized by *Brahman*-nature, which is of being consciousness and bliss in eternity.

In our understanding of the matter Shankara maintained that while from the empirical point of view, our thoughts about the ultimate Reality end up with the conception of the *Sagun Brahman* or the personal God, from the transcendental point of view our reflections suggest a complete identity between the soul and the *Brahman*. The liberated soul while still living realizes this truth in a mystical experience in which all consciousness of the subject-object distinction disappears and the world of plurality is transcended. In this philosophy all souls in their purity are considered one with *Brahman*. The consciousness of plurality or individual separate souls is considered to arise in the state of the universal soul's embodiment in different psycho-physical entities. When the truth is seen, it is realized that the plurality is only an illusion which is going to disappear completely in the final state of total absorption in the *Brahman*.

This view has been controversial. Shankara is charged of conflating the claim that in liberation the awareness of plurality disappears, with the claim that actual plurality ceases to exist (Frederick Copleston, *Religion and the One*, Search Press, London, 1982, p. 78). Does Shankara confuse the 'psychological' with the 'ontological'? I do not think so. Shankara is not saying that the Reality is actually plural and at the liberation of one soul the whole world as it were dissolves into *Brahman*. That would be too simplistic a claim to make for a great thinker like Shankara. Shankara's view is simply that in reality there is no pluralism. Pluralism exists only at the level of the 'psychological' actuality. It may be that Shankara's explanation of how the plurality comes to be manifest at a certain level of consciousness is philosophically not satisfactory. But he cannot be charged for confusing the issues. Once the distinction between the transcendental and the empirical consciousness is made, it becomes clear that there is no difference between 'being' and 'consciousness'. The latter is simply a mode of being. In any case from the point of religious fulfilment, it hardly matters whether the liberated soul loses its separate ontological status altogether or simply loses the consciousness of its separateness. This is so because the liberation is for eternity. And the reference to the soul, that is liberated, can be made only within the framework of temporality from the empirical point of view. The 'so and so' who is liberated is always one among the many so and so, known as such in the world of time and space. But since the consciousness of the universal *Brahman*-nature is gained for ever, his temporal identity has no religious significance.

Yet it is on this issue that other schools have differed from Shankara. The most famous "qualified non-dualist' is Ramanuja. He was a saint of devotional stream and died in A.D. 1127. He rejected the supra-personal view of Reality. He insisted on the personal nature of *Brahman* who is identical with the Creator, the *Ishwara*. Yet Ramanuja did not reject the thesis that in essence the human soul is 'non-different' from *Brahman*. He maintained that the world is the body of God. And god enters the human souls as their inner self. In Ramanuja's view *Brahman* is the soul, whose body includes the world as well as the individual souls. The body and soul cannot exist without each other. So the individual souls cannot exist apart from God, nor can God exist apart from the world and the individual souls. The bonded soul does not realize this truth. But the liberated soul does and enjoys the bliss of the 'whole'. Ramanuja sees Shankara to be preaching a total 'annihilation of the soul'. He maintains that "the ego is not simply an attribute of the (universal) Self . . . but constitutes the 'inward' nature of the Self . . . (which shines forth in the state of final release".[12]

Thus, the soul is not, strictly speaking, identical with *Brahman*. But since it is a 'part' of *Brahman*, in a sense it is one with *Brahman*. The liberated soul attains the consciousness of the *Brahman*-nature. It is absorbed in *Brahman*-consciousness. In a direct intuition the liberated soul is one with the supreme bliss of the *Brahman*-nature, though on the ontological level the released soul is not dissolved in God. Before Ramanuja, this point of view has been clearly stated in the *Brihadaranyaka Upanishad:*

> Dwelling in all things,
> Though other than all things,
> Who is not known by all things,
> Whose body all things are,
> He controls all things from within.[13]

Again, we can see that from the religious point of view in its soteriological significance, it hardly matters whether the soul retains its ontological separateness from *Brahman* or not. In one sense it does, in another sense it does not. In either case from religious point of view what matters is that the liberated soul is permanently imbued with the eternal blissful nature of God and he never returns to the world of birth and death, the *sansara*.

The third major stand on this issue maintains a strict Dualist or *Dvaita* position and a strictly theistic one. Its most vehement proponent is saint Madhva who lived in the thirteenth century A.D. In the Dualist position there is a sharp distinction between the human spirit and the ultimate reality which is personal and possesses all the attributes which we tend to ascribe to the one personal God or the Supreme Being. Madhva asserted the existence of a plurality of selves and things. In liberation the soul retains its separate individuality. The human soul is indestructible and when liberated it establishes a total communion with the divine spirit. It does not merge with the Divine spirit. It does not merge with the Divine but enjoys the truth, the goodness and the beauty of the eternal divine nature of God. For Madhva the plurality of souls is a matter of common experience. Memory bears witness to the separateness of my 'self' from other selves. The self as a subject of experiences is directly aware that all its experiences, including memory, are necessarily its own. All along, while it is conscious of other things in the world, the self is reflectively aware of itself, knowing itself to be one and the same individual throughout its changing biography. This dualism is famously asserted by the modern seer Sri Ramakrishna. He maintained that even during the enjoyment of the bliss of the knowledge of God, the individual retains his separateness. According to him, God leaves a little bit of 'I' in his devotee, even after giving him the knowledge of *Brahman*. Through that 'I' the devotee enjoys the infinite play of God. He retains the 'I' in order to taste the bliss of God and teach people accordingly. He has realized both aspects of God, personal and impersonal. This statement of the sage has been seen as his firm commitment to a Dualist position. But that is not true, since his statement is not meant to characterize the post-mortem state of fulfilment of the liberated soul. He is clearly talking about the embodied-liberated, i.e., the *jivanmukta*. And in this case it is perfectly understandable to claim that the devotee is simultaneously aware of the bliss of God and his embodied state as the individual 'I'. Moreover, from a religious point of view we must keep the question of the ontological status of the liberated soul separate from the question of its cognitive and connative fulfilment in the state of its union with God. And what is more important in religion is the latter. Concerning this there seems to be no disagreement between the three schools concerned. For Madhva too the union with God can be achieved while the soul is still embodied. And on death the disembodied soul is free for ever from further embodiments. And the soul's cognitive and connative fulfilment is characterized by his love of God and the experience of God's infinite and eternal nature as Truth, Goodness and Beauty.

As the *Yajurveda* puts it:

> He sees in all living beings
> The same soul as in himself
> And seeing the self
> As a part of the universal soul
> Does not consider anyone low
> He never hates anyone
> Nor falls victim to grief and sorrow.
> He is a lover of all
> An inseparable part of the universal joy.
> Flowing with the stream of Happiness
> He is enriched by all loving souls.[14]

At all times, however, the *Gita* remains the best source-book for understanding the Dualist's complex concept of freedom. In it we come across a unified and integrated view of the subject. It also introduces a new notion of freedom not found in earlier *Upanishadas*. It is the notion of '*Brahma-Nirvana*' or freedom-in-*Brahman*. The term *Brahman* is of *Upanishadic* origin. The essence of the *Upanishadic* teaching was given in the formula "*Tat tvam asi*" meaning 'That art Thou', suggesting that the true identity of the individual is the 'Universal Being'. And the term '*Nirvana*' is of Buddhist origin, signifying freedom as void or nothingness and freedom from rebirth. But *Brahma-Nirvana* signifies freedom constituted in the 'otherness' of being. It suggests that the individual is not lost in nothingness, but finds fulness in the infinity of being, which is of the nature of consciousness and bliss. In this it also goes beyond the conception of *Sankhya-yoga* school, which conceived of freedom as 'isolation' of the individual soul albeit in a blissful state of spiritual purity. Thus, the idea of freedom-in-*Brahman* represents a development upon all the three strands in Indian spirituality: the *Upanishadic*, the Buddhist and the *Sankhya-Yoga*. This is reflected well in the following verses of the *Gita:*

> One who has abandoned all
> Sensual desires and personal longings,
> Who is free from attachments and egoism
> He indeed receives true inner Peace.
> Such is the state of Brahmanhood
> Which attained one is not deluded.
> Even if attained in the last moment of life
> The attainer enters the *Brahma-Nirvana.*[15]

And later:

> Those who have destroyed the doubt within
> And are immersed in self-realization,
> Working always for the good of others,
> Free from evil intent
> They indeed attain to *Brahma-Nirvana.*[16]

Of all the seekers of *moksha*, those who have full religious knowledge of *Brahman* as well as the Supreme Being, are declared to be the greatest:

> Of all the seekers, the knower of *Brahman*,
> And the devotee of the Supreme Lord,
> Is the one, who holds Me the dearest
> And who is dearest to Me too.[17]

Perhaps, the most distinctive feature of *Brahma-Nirvana* is that it signifies the ontological richness of creativity. We know the *Brahman* is the ultimate; it is 'the one divine reality' of the *Rig Veda*. And we know that even the personal God is an emanation from *Brahman*. *Brahman* is the ultimate source of all creative energy. So freedom-in-*Brahman* clearly suggests that the *moksha*-realized individual, having transcended even the personality of God, becomes a participant in the creative process of *Brahman*. *Moksha* is, therefore, a dynamic, creative Absolute.

REFERENCES

1. *Rig Veda*, 7, 86, 5.
2. *Gita*, 2, 62-63.
3. *Ibid.*, 14, 19.
4. 7, 4.
5. 3, 27.
6. 2, 64.
7. *Gita*, 6, 29-30.
8. 9, 20-21.
9. *Gita*, 4, 9.
10. *The Brahma Sutra*, trs. S. Radhakrishnan, London, 1960.
11. *Vedanta Sutras* with commentary by Shankaracharya, 3, 4, 52.
12. *Vedanta Sutras* with commentary by Ramanuja, trs. G. Thibaut, p. 69f.
13. 3, 7, 15.
14. 40, 6.
15. 2, 71-72.
16. 5, 25.
17. *Gita*, 7, 17.

7

THE FOUR WAYS

DHYANA YOGA
THE WAY OF THE WILL AND DIRECTION OF MIND

One who acts without the desire.
For rewards is the true *Sanyasi*
The *Sanyasi* is the *Yogin*
Who has abandoned personal longings.[1]

Dhyana yoga as a method of contemplation is connected with the ancient practice of *yoga* proper. *Yoga* literally means 'yoking' or 'harnessing'. The ancient practice of *yoga* exemplified both these meanings. It is aimed at harnessing the power of nature to yoke on to the highest level of consciousness. In its later stage of development it was combined with the contemplation of the divine and grew into an integrated approach to God—Absolute-realization.

The practical aim of *Dhyana* is to achieve salvation through disciplined activity involving a thorough training by *hatha* or the effort of will, of both the body and the mind. The goal is to force a rupture of the human soul from its involvement with Nature so that it can rejoin the eternal and universal spirit. *Dhyana* literally means 'direction of the mind'. The discipline of *Dhyana* has three parts. Of these the first two, generally referred to as *Hatha Yoga*, are instrumental or preparatory to the third, the *Dhyana* proper. The first part deals with physical *asanas* or postures, which itself is popularly known as '*yoga*' outside India. The aim of these postures is either to keep fit a particular part of the body or to tone up the entire muscular system of the body. These postures have to be learnt through demonstration by an expert and have to be practised very accurately, or else they can produce harmful effects as well. There are some postures which are appended to what is called '*kriya*'. The aim of *kriyas* is to gain control of internal organs of the body to improve their efficiency and to keep them clean.

The second part of the discipline in question consists of what are called *pranayam*. The *pranayams* constitute a large body of basically breathing exercises. They are specially beneficial for the proper functioning of the circulatory system and the absorption of oxygen in the blood. *Pranayams* keep the nervous system and all the internal vital organs of the body, including the brain, in perfect condition. It helps to avoid all kinds of psycho-somatic diseases as well as the diseases caused by the malfunctioning of any of the various 'systems' of the body.

Given this background understanding of the physical aspect of *Dhyana yoga*, we can proceed to explain the specifically spiritual element of this path to God-realization. *Dhyana yoga* is directly connected with the ancient Indian practice of yoga conceived as a 'system' to attain command over Nature. The philosophy of this system was worked out much later (by second century B.C.) by Maharishi Patanjali in his work called *Yoga Sutras*. The essence of his philosophy is declared right in the beginning of this work:

> "*Yoga* is the control of the modifications of consciousness".[2]

What is achieved by this 'control' is the awakening of a spiritual power called *Kundalini* located in the human body. The *Kundalini* is represented as a snake coiled and seated at the base of the spine of the human body. There it lies dormant. But by the 'control of the modifications of consciousness', it wakes up and raises its head, and the psychic power lying dormant begins to flow upwards. From the base of the spine to the uppermost point in the brain it can flow to, there are seven psychic centres called *chakras*, located along the spine. The seventh *chakra*, called '*sahasra-padma*' (literally meaning 'thousand-petal-lotus'), is situated at the base of the brain. The awakening of this *chakra* is the ultimate fulfilment of *yoga*. First, by concentrating on the base of the spine, through a controlled consciousness, the aspirant's base-*chakra* is awakened. Then, under the skilful supervision of an adept *yogin*, the flow of the *Kundalini*-energy is regulated to flow upwards, passing one by one through various higher *chakras* and awakening them, until (rarely) the highest *chakra* is awakened.

It is a very carefully guided exercise, since things can also go wrong. The flow of energy can take a downward path bringing evil powers to the aspirant. The aspirant can get 'locked' into these powers and enter demonic abodes. For such a thing not to happen, the *guru* of the aspirant has to make sure that this disciple's *karmic* background is 'clean'. The *guru* has also to monitor the movement of the *Kundalini* and has to be able to interfere with it and stop the wrong movements. With each *chakra*, except the last one, there rests a special psychic power which the aspirant is able to harness as he moves along the path towards the highest. With each *chakra* also, including the highest one, the aspirant is able to connect with its specific plane of consciousness manifesting a world of its own. Thus, there are worlds within worlds. With the highest *chakra* the story is different. It does not represent a particular world or a specific power. When the highest *chakra* is awakened, consciousness, as we know it with the conceptual mind, wholly disappears. Consciousness, as we normally know it, is ego-centred and structured in time. Such consciousness is individualistic and there is always, atleast vestigially, some self-awareness accompanying all states of consciousness. But with the awakening of the *sahasra-padma* the individual's ego-consciousness is absorbed into the pure universal consciousness.

One wonders now, what its spiritual significance is! What is so attractive about losing one's individual consciousness into the abyss of the universal consciousness? The answer is that in this respect *yoga* appears to be the precursor of the doctrine of non-dualism as advocated by Shankara. As we have seen in the earlier chapters, Shankara distinguished between the *Nirgun-Brahman* and the *Sagun-Brahman* and characterized the former as 'Being, Consciousness and Bliss'. He also maintained that in the ultimate analysis the individual soul is one with the *Brahman*. It is this state of unity with the *Brahman* which is *Dhyana Yoga* the *yogin* achieves through his own efforts by the deliberate control of consciousness. The *yogin* can get into and get out of this state of unity at will. But he can also affect this unity permanently at will. The *yogi,* whose *sahasra-padma* is awakened, is supposed to have acquired the power to unite with *Brahman* at will permanently, resulting in the wilful death of his body. And this, as we have seen, is one positive fulfilment of the state of eternal freedom or *moksha*. Further, this willed death resulting in the soul's unity with the *Brahman* is also the momentous event signifying the total ending of the cycle of rebirths for the *yogin*. And this, as we have seen, is the fulfilment of the material aspect of the goal of *moksha*.

But there is a theistic side to *Dhyana Yoga* as well. Though Patanjali himself does not invoke a personal God as the Creator, he does introduce the worship of a personal God considered as the universal Teacher. The Lord is seen as the eternal Spirit, untouched by *karma* and not existing in time. As the *Sutra* tells us:

> *Ishwara* (i.e., God) is a Unique Spirit,
> He is unaffected by suffering,
> Or *Karma*, or the merits and demerits
> Of *Karma*, or the perceptions (of the senses).
> He is the knower of all in its essence,
> He was the *guru* of the ancient sages,
> And he is not confined in time.[3]

The worship of the Lord is supposed to help the practice of the 'control of consciousness'. Meditations on the Lord's sublime perfections is supposed to purify the mind of the seeker. All along, however, Patanjali emphasizes the following of certain rules of conduct including both mental and physical observances. These are called *Yama* and *Niyama*. There are five *Yamas:* non-violence, truthfulness, self-denial, celibacy and renunciation. *Niyamas* recommended are also five in number: internal cleanliness, contendedness, austerity, penance and meditation on God.

In Hinduism, however, the theistic interpretation of *Dhyana Yoga* receives full attention. Yoga bypasses the *kundalini* practices of the original *yoga*. It recommends concentration on the mental image of a personal God and meditation on the attributes of the sacred symbol '*OM*' or, alternatively, on the name of God. And also, 'God' is taken in the full sense, including his power as the Creator. The state of a self-realized *yogin* is described in the *Gita* as follows:

> Having shunned the enjoyment
> Of the outer (material) pleasures,
> Establishing his vision internally
> Between the eye-brows,
> Keeping the breath steady,
> The senses, thoughts and the intellect controlled
> Freed from desire, fear and anger
> The *yogin* attains to *moksha* while still alive.[4]

The true *yogin*, it is said, is the one who has conquered desire, who is at peace with himself, who is equal-minded in the conditions of pleasure as well as pain and who is unflattered by obeisance and unhurt by insults. And further it is said:

> The one who is fulfilled
> By his knowledge and experience
> Who is unmoved by temptations
> And has full control over the senses.
> The one who is unimpaired by poverty or riches
> Such a man is indeed a true *yogin*.[5]

In all cases, however, there is great emphasis on inner renunciation and the control of consciousness.

> Having stilled his consciousness,
> Renouncing pleasure and accumulation of wealth
> Staying alone in quiet ambience.
> The *yogin* joins his soul with the Supreme Spirit.[6]

KARMAYOGA

Karmayoga takes a complete ethical perspective upon life. In day to day life only sometimes our duties are in concord with our personal likes and dislikes, but more often than not what our duties demand are not the same as what one would like to do in the given situation. It is not hard to see why this is like that. Man is basically self-seeking. And since the material resources, which bring him personal satisfaction, are generally obtained through competition they are bound to involve some or the other form of deprivation of others. Sometimes one's own position may be better 'justified'. But then generally, again, the criterion of 'justified' itself has built-in preferences for the dominant class. As against this self-seeking perspective upon life, the ethical perspective demands a wholly impartial attitude. The *Karmayoga* is the discipline which helps you develop this outlook as a part of your permanent personality. This means living one's life in the observance of one's duties. And this in turn requires a spiritual development in which one attains a consciousness of a discriminative 'selflessness'. Acting from this background of selflessness is the *Karmayogi*'s way of being in the world. And through this way of living one attains to perfection. As it is said in the *Gita:* "Each man who is devoted to the performance of his duties attains perfection. And let me explain how he attains *moksha* while he is engaged in performing his own duties.

The one, from whom all beings have evolved and by whom all this is pervaded; worshipping that one with the performance of his duties, man attains perfection".[7]

Karmayoga thus is not just conformity to the readymade 'duties' currently accepted and recommended by the society. It needs a great power of discernment of what exactly is one's duty in a given situation, for every general statement of a duty needs interpretation in a given situation in the light of particular facts of the case. This needs a discriminative mind which is enlightened and which has insight into the nature of society and which has understanding of one's own passions and the self-seeking tendencies. Next, it needs actual, not merely an 'intellectual', disengagement from the self-centered dispositions of man. In the *Gita* this motivational disinvestment is called 'non-attachment'. Let us see how the *Gita* unfolds the idea of non-attachment which enables a man to live the life of a *Karmayogi*.

We can approach the subject by contrasting it with the phenomenon of 'attachment'. Attachment seems to be the very basis of the psychological continuity of life. It connects the human self, his desires and emotions with his actions and his plans for his future achievements.

> Attached by hundreds of ties of desire
> Given to lust and anger
> They strive to amass wealth, by
> Unjust means for their gratification.
> 'This today has been gained by me:
> This desire I shall attain,
> This is mine and that shall also be mine'.
> 'This foe is slain by me
> And others also I shall slay.
> I am the lord, the enjoyer,
> I am the successful, mighty and happy'.
> Bewildered by many thoughts,
> Entangled in the meshes of delusion,
> Addicted to gratification of desires,
> They fall into a foul hell.[8]

I think it will be generally agreed that the psychology of action, described above, is pretty much universal. It is very well exemplified in the contemporary scenario. Basically what it maintains is that desire, being the inner stimulus for action, leads to attachment and self-fulfilment is its rationale. This significance of desire is one of the oldest discoveries of the sages. It is asserted in the earliest Hindu scripture of the *Rig Veda:*

> Desire first stirred up the world
> Desire was the organised seed of the spirit.
> The connection of the existent
> To the nonexistent,

> Which the sages found,
> Searching in their hearts with wisdom.[9]

Now if human life is action-based and actions have their source fundamentally in desires, then *prima facie* a plea for non-attachment, by contrast, would appear to be a recommendation for inaction. Indeed, it amounts to a negation of life itself. The *Gita* itself rightly notes that in human life action, both mental and bodily, is necessary and inevitable:

> For no one even for a moment
> Can remain without action.
> Helplessly all are driven to action
> By the impulses born of nature.[10]

Any account of non-attachment, therefore, must be sensitive to the apparent conflict between non-attachment and the necessity of action. And it must also show how actions, if at all possible without attachment, would prove to be worthwhile in respect of self-fulfilment and human perfection. And it must face the materialist squarely who asserts:

"You ignorant boy, such are the fooleries of these unenlightened men. They conceive that you ought to throw away the pleasures of life because they are mixed with pain; but what prudent man will throw away unpeeled rice which encloses excellent grain because it is covered with the husk".[11]

The Hindu understanding of non-attachment is best presented in a dialogue in the *Gita*, between Krishna and his warrior-friend Arjuna, in the battle of Kurukshetra. When all is set and the battle is going to begin, Arjuna is struck with grief at the thought of gaining victory by killing his own teachers, friends and kinsmen, who happen to be in the opposite camp. Feeling shattered and emotionally distraught Arjuna lays down his weapons and proposes to relinquish his claim to the kingdom, which he is supposed to defend in the battle:

> O'Lord! In killing my own people
> I do not see any glory.

> By killing them I do not wish victory
> Nor do I desire the kingdom and its pleasures.[12]

And this is where Krishna initiates Arjuna in the philosophy of non-attachment. Krishna maintains that not only action is inevitable, but the right action is also the way to perfection and finally to *moksha*. And the right action is characterized as the action performed in non-attachment, which in turn is explained as an action performed not for any motive of personal gain, but with the sole motive of doing one's duty in the given circumstances. In one famous verse of the *Gita* Krishna says:

> To action alone thou has a right
> And never at all to its fruits.
> Let not the fruits of action be thy motive
> Nor let there be in thee any attachment to inaction.[13]

And later connecting non-attachment with *moksha*, Krishna says:

> One who has put aside pride and longings
> Who has removed the ills arising from attachment
> Who is still in himself and calm in his passions
> Who is free from the conflicts of pleasure and pain
> Such a self-knowing man
> Reaches out to the abode of the Eternal.[14]

Non-attachment thus is essentially a state of inner freedom from the compulsions of the self-seeking desires. Far from being an exemplar of 'inaction', non-attachment is the prime fulfilment of the truly ethical consciousness. For, action flowing from non-attachment is completely free from the motive of self-gratification. In non-attachment the actor performs his deeds solely for realizing the highest good which the situation calls for. The good he aims at is good for all. It is something intrinsically good. As in the case of Arjuna, Krishna urges him to fight for the sake of realizing the righteous order of justice. He is not to fight for a personal gain of kingdom or glory.

O Arjuna! surrendering all works to Me
Being aware of My spiritual nature
Remaining disinterested in profit and ownership
Without attachment and laziness fight the war.[15]

In the normal course of our upbringing our minds get thoroughly conditioned in the values of the social milieu of our times. We are attached to those values and the traditions which embody them. And we blindly conform to the so-called 'duties' required to be performed by us. A conditioned mind cannot be truly impartial. It cannot perceive the 'truth of the situation' and therefore cannot resolve the ethical dilemma of the kind Arjuna is faced with. Only through non-attachment one is able to have a fresh look at the situation and able to choose the right action in the light of what is objective and what is universally valid. Krishna admonishes Arjuna for his weakness of the will. He characterizes Arjuna's state of mind as of *moha*, i.e., sentimental attachment. Such a state of mind blurs one's discriminative abilities and blinds one to seeing his true duties in the given situation. Krishna makes Arjuna realize that a righteous war must be fought independently of the considerations of personal gain or loss. This war is righteous, since it aims at justice which is the very foundation of human society. Therefore, Arjuna in his status as a warrior-prince has a moral duty to fight such a war. In this he must ignore the demands of his attachments. And even though, as a matter of fact, fighting this war will bring Arjuna personal gain, he must not fight for the sake of these gains. To maintain its distinctively moral worth he must fight with the motive of duty alone, this he can do only if he has come out of the state of *moha* into the state of non-attachment.

Non-attachment must also be distinguished from the ascetic practice of 'detachment'. Detachment signifies a consolidation of the power of the will, which can be ruthlessly applied to attain a particular personal goal without any regard for other people's interest in the ethical perspective. Detachment involves an unhealthy suppression of desires and emotions. In it there is no freedom from the motive of the 'me-aspect of actions'. It is only that all effort is concentrated upon a particular (personal) gain, subordinating to it all other demands of human relationship. But non-attachment is not realized in this way; it is a religious and ethical achievement. It is attained through the grace of God by realizing the spiritual nature of the soul and its ultimate good in its return to *Brahman* in *moksha*. That is, one has firstly to realize that in itself the soul is of the same essence as *Brahman*, i.e., of Being, Consciousness and Bliss. And then, that living one's life in the pursuit of personal glory and successes keeps one implicated in the order of rebirths and the world of sorrow. And thirdly, that freedom from the round of rebirth is the ultimate good of human existence. Then, such a person, quite spontaneously, attains non-attachment. The simple wisdom of these realizations enables him to, inwardly, jettison the motive of personal gain from the intention to perform the action, for the sake of duty alone. He is, then living his life like a *Karmayogi*.

It now remains to be seen how the way of *karma* leads to the ultimate goal of *moksha*. *Gita*'s explanation is contained in the following passages:

> Apart from work done as and for Duty
> This life is in bondage to work
> So, O Kauntey! act in the spirit of sacrifice
> Be free from all attachments.[16]
> Those who live their lives in non-attachment
> Only they attain to *Moksha* through works.[17]

What is being suggested here is that the work done in the spirit of sacrifice, i.e., without the motive of personal gain, does not lead to the accumulation of the merits and demerits of *karma*. We have seen that *karma*, through both good and bad deeds, keeps the soul implicated in the round of rebirths. But the person who lives a life of non-attachment to the fruits of works does not, in fact, earn any merit or demerit required by a rebirth.

As the *Gita* declares:

> One who has abandoned the fruits of actions
> Who is always contended and not dependent

He though living an active life of works
Is not considered as the doer of actions.[18]

And further:

He who is even-minded through profit and loss
Who has transcended the life of conflicts and envy
Who is calm in both success and failure
He, though engaged in works, is not enslaved by it.[19]

And giving the example of his own life Krishna in the *Gita* stresses the point:

O Dhananjaya! the works do not bind me to the world.
I live disinterested and unattached to them.[20]

Finally, *Karmayoga* adopts a thoroughly theistic perspective. The active life of works without the motive of personal gain is not a mere moral exercise; it is not just a matter of ascetic detachment to gain moral perfection. Throughout his life the *Karmayogi* is open to a real relationship with God. His non-attachment is linked to religious attitudes. A *Karmayogi* seeks *moksha* through the grace of God. No doubt, the *Karmayoga* emphasizes motiveless action, but it also emphasizes the devotional aspects of religion. He acts as though his actions are offerings to God. And so, in the *Gita* the Lord promises:

Those who surrender their works to Me
And worship Me with unwavering sentiments
Who fix their mind and heart on Me throughout their works
Them I save quickly from the ocean of life and death.[21]

BHAKTI
(THE PATH OF LOVE OF GOD)

One who sees Me manifest
Acknowledging everything in Me

I am never lost to him
Nor is he lost to Me.[22]

The term '*bhakti*' is hard to translate into one word in English. It represents a complex concept connoting love, devotion and faith. The tradition of religious devotion or the *Bhaktiyoga* is as old as the *Rig Veda*.

Do your duties and leave
The rest to God
Having deep faith in His justice.
The world is torn by conflicts,
Enmities and competition,
In this dark whirlpool of
Tumultous stream of life;
Only the omnipotent God
May help you go across the ocean of turmoils . . .
Only with His blessing
You can conquer the troubles
Through his divine grace.[23]

But it was pretty much entrenched in the Indian spiritual philosophies by the time of the writing of the *Bhagvad Gita*, which offers a magnificent literary expression of the notion. It has encouraged creation of temples where an image of the Lord is worshipped by the devotees. The Hindu worship in the temples usually takes the form of chantings of sacred syllables, singing devotional songs, dancing in front of the idols, contemplation and various sacraments. The most popular sacrament is *bhoga* (akin to the Christian Eucharist) in which a variety of items of food are consecrated and consumed. The *bhakti* movement through its various forms of worship has considerably influenced the course of the development of art, music, architecture and literature in all the religions of India.

However, worship in the temples is not essential to the embrace of *bhakti*. Rather, a true follower of this path tends to avoid the rituals and the rites performed in the temples. He seeks direct access to the Lord without the mediation of the priests. The highest goal for a *bhakta* (i.e., the follower of *bhakti*) is to seek a mystical unity with the Lord in the form of a merger with God's universal consciousness.

In his approach the *bhakta* attains a stage where his consciousness of self-disappears and there remains simply the unmanifest and the inward reality of the Divine presence. In this the devotee does not seek a vision of the anthropomorphic image of God. The love of the *bhakta* leads him to an absorption in the beloved God. As Kabir, the poet-saint of the fifteenth century, has written:

> When it is I,
> Thou is not
> When Thou reveals in me
> The I dissolves;
> The lane of love
> Is too narrow
> For both You and I
> To promenade.

All the same, the *bhaktas* of a God—incarnate, especially of Rama or Krishna insist on experiencing a divine manifestation or theophany of the embodied form in which they imagine their Lord to have actually existed and roamed around in the world. The great saints such as Meera Bai, Surdas and Ramakrishna and others are popularly believed to have seen Krishna with their human eyes. The result of such encounters with God is, however, that, through the grace of God, their *karmic* sins are dissolved and they attain *jivanmukti*, i.e., release from the round of rebirths while still living on earth.

> Those who engage in Me
> And worship Me in love
> To them I give spiritual knowledge
> With which they, in turn, find Me
> With compassion I kindle
> The flame of wisdom in their hearts

And destroy the darkness
Of ignorance therby.[24]

Both these strands of bhakti, however, enjoin the ultimate spiritual illumination which brings, by the grace of god, a deep inner transformation in the *bhakta's* psyche. His love of God takes over the command of his life and dissolves his consciousness of separation from the divine. His love of God is imbued with the passion and commitment of faith.

And of a man of faith the Lord speaks thus:

A man of faith, immersed in faith
With senses controlled attains knowledge
And knowledge attained, he quickly
Finds the highest Peace.
But the ignorant man, having no faith
Goes doubting to self-destruction
For the doubting self, there is neither
This world, nor the other, nor joy.[25]

Faith is a complex notion signifying a total inner surrender to God. Surrender is not just a matter of holding a set of religious beliefs in an unshakable manner and going through the motion of worship. The objectification of faith is quite contrary to the inwardness and commitment of faith which Kierkegaard has rightly described as "the highest passion in the sphere of human subjectivity". Thus in the *Gita*, Krishna tells Arjuna: "God is residing in the heart of all beings . . . surrender to Him in all your sentiments, and you will be blessed with supreme Peace and the abode of the eternal".[26]

And later in the same place in the *Gita*, speaking in the capacity of God-Incarnate, Krishna says to Arjuna:

Have faith in Me, with devotion,
Offering works, salute Me
You will reach Me, you are dear to Me
This is My true promise to you
Abandoning all traditional duties

> Come to my refuge alone.
> I will free you from all your sins
> And lead you into *moksha*, do not lament.[27]

The nature of the inner surrender has to be understood properly. Surely, the surrender in question is the surrender of the 'self' which is the owner of all one's experiences and the doer of all one's actions. So the surrender of the self would involve a total ending of all the manifestations of attachment—the will to personal power, wealth and fame, and the whole sense of personal achievement or 'becoming' through which the self sustains its feeling of continuity as the same 'I'. Thus, surrender will bring an end to the feeling of separation of man from the divine. To surrender is to die to one's self seeking attachments and thus be free from the *karmic* involvement in the desire for personal fulfilment.

Now, it is clear that a surrender of the self cannot be achieved by an act of will involving mental effort alone. The will is an instrument of self-assertion and the manipulations of the self. Therefore, the self cannot deliberately and self-consciously set about to achieve its own surrender by willing. It seems then that surrender can come about only in an act of utter simplicity, in total spontaneity of a motiveless love of God. One has to approach the matter indirectly.

Perhaps, one can resolve to fulfil the necessary conditions for surrender to happen in one's life. That is what is suggested in the *Gita:*

> Engaged in the quest of *Brahman*, keeping cheerful,
> Not lamenting, putting aside personal ambitions,
> One who lives in total impartiality to all beings,
> Receives the supreme blessing of *bhakti* of Me.[28]

It is clear from the above words of Krishna that true *bhakti* is something which arises in man spontaneously, when he has lived a life of ethical impartiality, spiritual non-attachment and discriminative knowing of *Brahman*. The path of love of God, therefore, enjoins the elements of all the other three modes of the

Hindu pursuit of God (Perhaps that is why, it is discussed in the last chapter in the *Gita*). It is most significant that the Lord has himself taken care to deliver the deep meaning of *bhakti* to mankind. For it is only too easy for man to convince himself, self-deceptively that he has received the blessing of *bhakti*, since he is performing laboriously all the rituals of worship. It is to harbour the illusion of *bhakti*, for it gives such a (false) sense of security and escape from the sorrows and the harsh realities of life. So man is advised not to become a recluse and renounce the world but to renounce only the attachment to the fruits of his works. In this way he surrenders to God 'in all his sentiments' without any reservations in favour of his personal ambitions etc. Thus Krishna explains:

> My true devotee works as though
> Under my supervision, remaining engaged
> In the works of life as usual, he, by my grace,
> Finds the eternal and indestructible status.[29]

To fulfil the necessary conditions for receiving the grace of *bhakti*, therefore, requires the choice of a whole way of life which is absolutely selfless and open to the grace of God. It is a life which is lived not only in a contemplative and worshipful consciousness of the divine presence, but also in an active engagement with life in the spirit of service of God. And thus Lord Krishna speaks of the true devotee of God:

> And of all the seekers, the one
> Who with great faith always
> Abides in Me, thinks of Me
> Within himself and renders
> Motiveless loving service to Me,
> He is the most intimately united with Me
> In *yoga* and is the highest of all.[30]

GYAṆA MARG
(THE WAY OF SPIRITUAL KNOWLEDGE)

The way of spiritual knowledge
Now I will explain again
The truth Supreme in all knowledge
Knowing which the seekers of Truth
Have found the highest spiritual abode.[31]

In Hinduism meditation is believed to be the key to the attainment of spiritual knowledge. And spiritual knowledge or Truth-realization is the perfect way to *moksha.* There are three focii for the conduct of meditation, giving rise to three forms of meditative approaches to the ultimate Reality. These are vested in God, the universal Self and the existential self. Of these the first is best discovered in the *Gita.* Though all the ways to *moksha* are discussed in the *Gita,* it is maintained that the way of 'steady wisdom' is the best. A man of steady wisdom lives a life of great spiritual discipline and eventually experiences the Eternal.

He is free from the ego and greed
He has no hatred for anyone
He is patient and even minded in sorrow and joy
He is amicable and full of compassion.[32]

It is clear from the above verse that the character of the discipline involved in spiritual knowledge is not that of asceticism. One does not become free from egoism and greed, and 'full of compassion', through ascetic practices. What is required is not the suppression of desires and emotions, but freedom from these through 'steady wisdom'.

One who has made the inner-renunciation,
Is free from the vices of attachment,
Is ever established in the bliss of the soul,
Whose desires are pacified,
Who is free from the conflicts of pleasure and pain,
Such a knower of the Spiritual receives the everlasting abode.[33]

This knowledge of the Spirit comes only through 'pure' meditation. The *Gita* explains the idea of pure meditation as follows:

"In pure meditation, the meditator has no motive of personal, individual gain whatsoever. In it he approaches God with an understanding of the divine nature, and for the sake of knowing God alone. There are four types of motives with which a person may approach God. These are: to relieve one's suffering; for intellectual curiosity; for some material gain or for spiritual knowledge. Of these the seeker of the spiritual knowledge is the highest and dearest to God. He is the highest because he understands that there is nothing better than the status of Freedom-in-God. After many lives of engagement in pure meditation the seeker finds God. Such a *mahatma*, who knows God as omnipresent, is indeed rare".[34] Again as Krishna explains: "Those who worship gods of the heaven receive only the gains which they worship them for. What these dim-minded people receive is ephemeral. They do not know of My eternal nature, and think that the gains of the senses are the highest. I am covered by My power of self-manifestation, and the ignorant world does not know Me as the unborn, and the indestructible".[35]

We know in ordinary experience that we do not always approach God for the sake of spiritual knowledge. Covertly, even the Supreme Being is approached for some or the other worldly gain for self-gratification. What Krishna is saying is that in pure meditation upon God, one has to put aside all motives except the pure motive of spiritual knowledge for its own sake. Or else, one would not find the absolute truth, but only some 'illusion' which will gratify the ignorant ego. Indeed, it is said that in a total encounter with Truth one is so totally transformed that one loses one's ego-centric personal consciousness altogether, and the 'I' is confined to a merely need-centered awareness of self-interest. And this stands to reason. We know that our beliefs condition our desires and actions. The beliefs, based in the ignorance of God, condition our minds to seek self-gratification. So when, in the perception of Truth, those beliefs are destroyed, it is to be expected that there will be freedom from "the conflicts of pleasure and pain" and from "the ego and greed".

In the *Gita*, meditation upon God requires the realization that the Supreme Being is the manifest counterpart of the unmanifest *Brahman*. It requires the recognition of both the *nirguna* and *saguna* aspects of God as the unitary ultimate reality. Indeed, it requires one to meditate upon the God of the *Upanishadas*.

> The highest, the ultimate
> Who is hidden in all beings
> Respective to their bodies,
> The One who encompasses the universe
> Realizing Him as Lord
> The *yogin* becomes immortal.[36]

In pure meditation one takes refuge in the Lord and in that act of deep surrender one finds the eternal.

> All are attracted to the three forms of attributes.
> (Virtue, Power and Pleasure)
> So they do not know Me the supreme, eternal.
> Difficult is to go beyond the three-fold manifestations
> But those who take refuge in Me reach the Eternal.[37]

Further, it is maintained that only in a full encounter with Reality, one is able to break away from the chains of *karma*. "A person may abstain from sense objects but the sense objects do not leave him from being desired. But when a person experiences the higher Reality he receives freedom from desires".[38]

Furthermore, in the *Gita*, it has been made very clear that whatever way or *yoga* one adopts to find God, in the end it is spiritual knowledge of the hidden essence of God that alone liberates the soul into *moksha*.

> As the wood is reduced
> To ashes by the heat of the fire
> So the fire of knowledge brings to ashes all accumulated *karma*.
> In this world, nothing
> Purifies better than spiritual knowledge,

It is the ultimate realized
In time through *Gyan* Yoga,
The way that leads to the Self within.[39]

Similarly, the *Atharaveda* proclaims:

And he who goes deeper
Into the self and sees
The strings of life-forces
Bringing together the person
Into a unity
Knows the real being.
Such a knower sees
The great omnipotent and
The omnipresent God,
Who is immanent and
Transcendent to all compounded
Entities of the infinite universe.
Go deeper to find the ultimate truth.[40]

So in the *Gita*, *Gyanyoga* is not wholly separated from *Bhaktiyoga*. The growth of higher knowledge contributes to the deepening of devotional consciousness and the higher achievements of devotion brings about a total absorption in truth-consciousness. This is to be expected, for the knowledge of the spiritual truth is not a merely intellectual matter. On the path of the spiritual knowledge thought, emotion and action must move together. It requires a recognition of the limitations of the human mind and therefore a surrender to the immensity of God. It is not a matter of ambition but a reverential 'openness' to enable one to receive the Truth. And these are, as we have seen, proper devotional attitudes. Spiritual knowledge is a matter of illumination of the mind and a disclosure of being in the purity of human heart. To approach God with this purity of heart is true devotion and pure meditation. This the *Gita* states clearly:

Those who taking refuge in Me
Attempt to free themselves from rebirth

> They surely gain, the complete.
> Knowledge of *Brahman*, spirituality and action.[41]

From the above explanation of spiritual knowledge we may conclude that the following seven discriminative truths constitute the core of Hindu enlightenment:

1. That God is seated in the heart of all beings.
2. That human life is regulated by the instrument of *maya* or attachment.
3. That freedom from attachment comes by putting aside the desire of the fruits of action.
4. That the 'I' is not the doer of actions, it is the *gunas* acting on *gunas*.
5. The true self is universal, is the "witness" or the "silent presence" to all the events in the universe.
6. That 'surrender' to God in your heart, in all your sentiments, brings peace and wisdom.
7. By the grace of God perfect spiritual knowledge is born and thereby *moksha* is attained.

RAMANA MAHARSHI— WHO AM I? (MEDITATION ON THE UNIVERSAL SELF)

In our times Ramana Maharshi is considered to be the most profound attainer of the *Upanishadic* goal of self-realization. In self-realization the individuality of the 'self' is seen to be illusory and the meditator becomes consciously aware of his true identity as the universal Self or Spirit. This is claimed to be the highest experiential spiritual knowledge bringing to an end the long chain of rebirths and liberating the individual into *moksha* at his final demise.

The Maharshi's meditation centres around the enquiry "Who am I?" It is important to realize that it is not a merely theoretical inquiry as in philosophy. Its practical nature is what concerns us here especially. Historically Maharshi's own meditation was set in when he experienced an unaccountable, sudden, violent fear of death. The Maharshi, still only seventeen years old, without any sickness, one day just felt very strongly that he was going to die. This prompted him to actually find out what is meant to die. But since the first-hand experience of death while still alive was not available to him, he feigned the conditions of physical death as well as he could, "I lay with my limbs stretched out stiff as though *rigor mortis* had set in and imitated a corpse so as to give greater reality to the inquiry. I held my breath and kept my lips tightly closed so that no sound could escape, so that neither the word 'I' nor any other word could be uttered. Well then, I said to myself, this body is dead".[42]

But now something extraordinary happened to the Maharshi. In a sudden flash of illumination the Maharshi could perceive his transcendental identity with "deathless spirit". This means that he actually experienced death as we normally conceive of it, i.e., as a total loss of the sense of embodiment. In his own description Maharshi is careful to distinguish this experience from a mere feat of imagination. "All this was not dull thought; it flashed through me vividly as living truth which I perceived directly almost without thought-process".[43]

And as the proof of the pudding is in the eating, from that time onwards, the Maharshi's consciousness of his identity with the universal self continued unbroken. From that time onwards the Maharshi continued to live on both the empirical and the transcendental planes simultaneously. He would perform the functional duties of his daily life in the material world, while all along remaining aware of his immaterial being in the universal spirit. He never relapsed into the state of ignorance of the spirit, never lost his timeless transcendence to the temporal limitations of the empirical ego. This point can be clearly understood by the following most perceptive comment of the Maharshi. Once when the Maharshi in the state of acute pain was actually wailing, his disciples wondered how could the self-realized soul be at all feeling pain! The Maharshi explained to them that, 'it is not me who is in pain but rather the pain is in me'.

In one stroke the Maharshi had clearly distinguished his essence both from the physical body as well as from the mental attributes which inhere the body. Like Shankara, he maintained that the world was created by the power of thought. And the power of thought is itself vested in the holy spirit. In the final analysis the reality is one, the universal Self. And the individual egos with all the drama of their lives are constituted by thought emanating from the Spirit. In a self-realized individual, like the Maharshi, the play of thought goes on until his physical death, but the individual is not taken in by it. Knowing his true ontological status as the supreme Spirit, he sees not only his own mind but the minds of all others, as existing in his own true being. Thus, both the wailings and the ecstasies manifested by the body are all in him, he is not feeling them because he is not identified with them, like a wave is in the ocean but the ocean is not identified with the wave. The Maharshi was also careful to explain that the world is both real and unreal depending on the observer's perspective. From the transcendental point of view, the world is unreal in the sense that it has no reality independently of the supporting Self, but in the empirical perspective, the world is real in the sense that to a normal observer located in time and space, who is ignorant of the one ultimate spirit, the world would appear to be a separate, self-subsistent reality. Again, with regard to the existence of a personal God, the Maharshi's doctrine is similar to that of non-Dualism or *Advaita* of Shankara. The personal God is the ultimate reality if the Absolute is conceived by the mind. But for the man of self-realization, who has a supramental direct intuition of the Supreme Spirit, personal God is only as real as the world. Further, though the Maharshi taught a method of inquiry into oneself, he attached little importance to the theoretical knowledge of the scriptures or the rituals and the rites of an organized religion, and conspicuously discouraged speculative inquiry into spiritual matters. His positive practical concern with spirituality can be clearly discerned in his reply to a disciple who inquired about the post-mortem condition of the human soul. Pointedly he answered, 'Why did he want to know what he would be after death when he did not even know what he was in this life'? The message is clear: 'Find out for yourself what you are now and the rest will become known by itself'.[44]

All the same, he tended to recommend different practices to different individuals, according to their own temperaments and commitments. To a passionate devotee of the personal God, he recommended the method of 'total surrender'. It involves the faith that the individual ego is not the 'doer' of the activities one performs in his daily living, because everything happens according to God's will. Why not give up being the doer and the chooser then and let one's life be guided by the supreme will! In total surrender one lives with this understanding and leaves everything for God to take care of. The Maharshi explains his point by the example of an ignorant man who travels in a train, but still keeping his luggage on his head. The traveller does not realize that his luggage would be equally carried by the train itself. The worshipper of the personal God should realize that God is the bearer of all the burdens of this life. And with this realization he should surrender to God completely.

However, the Maharshi was absolutely clear in his view that to find the absolute Truth, the universal Self, there is no other method than 'enquiry'. Though, until the mind becomes established in itself, some kind of *Bhavana* (contemplation of a personified god or goddess with deep emotion and religious feeling) is essential. Otherwise, the mind will be frequently assailed by wayward thoughts or sleep.[45] But eventually the mind must 'attain effortlessly its natural state of freedom from concepts' and then the sense of 'I' and 'mine' are gone completely. The practice of '*bhavanas*', therefore, is useful only at the initial stages, and should not be indulged into with the desire of receiving paranormal powers from the deity. And so soon as sufficient mental strength is attained, one should proceed to pursue the method of inquiry into oneself.

In the practice of inquiry asceticism is not recommended. Instead, 'moderation in food, moderation in sleep and moderation in speech' are considered necessary. The path of actual inquiry consists of a meditative conscious negation of one's identity with any of the elements of the body and mind. The Maharshi explains it as the process of inwardly dissociating one's self-awareness from its identification with the functions of the gross body and the bodily humours, the five cognitive sense-organs as well as from the functions of breathing and thinking. Nor should one consider oneself as 'nescience' devoid of substantiality and being-consciousness.

In this way the world which is merely 'what-is-seen' (as what is perceived by the mind) will be removed from consciousness and there will be the realization of the self which is the true seer. After negating all the mental representations in consciousness, there remains simply the pure awareness, which the Maharshi claims, what 'I truly am'. The Self is the substratum of the world; its true knowledge can arise only when the false has been put aside. The seer and the object seen are related in the same manner as the rope and the illusory perception of the rope as a snake. When the illusion goes the knowledge of the real manifests by itself. The illusion will disappear with the inquiry 'Who is it that sees them'? Just as one sees a drama on the cinema screen without thinking of oneself as seeing the real happenings, so should one proceed with negating one's identity with the seer, and the sufferer or the enjoyer of the world of the senses. Eventually, one would be left only with the universal Self in whom is constituted all the seeing, the enjoying and the suffering. If one has gone that far one is no longer deluded by the subject-object dualism. The universal Self is both the subject and the object. When there is no separation then there is neither the worldly suffering nor the worldly pleasure. Then there is only the supreme bliss, the eternal non-dual awareness.

"When one is engaged in various empirical acts there should be the firm conviction 'I am the Self', without allowing the false idea 'I am the body etc.' to rise. If the mind should stray away from its state, then immediately one should inquire, 'Oh! Oh! We are not the body etc.! Who are we?, and thus one should reinstate the mind in that (pure) state. The inquiry 'Who am I?' is the principal means to the removal of all misery and the attainment of the supreme bliss. When in this manner the mind becomes quiescent in its own state, self-experience arises of its own accord, without any hindrance. Thereafter sensory pleasures and pains will not affect the mind. All (phenomena) will appear, then, without attachment like a dream".[46]

J. KRISHNAMURTI—I

J. Krishnamurti is well-known for his critique of organized religion. To some people it amounts to a rejection of religion altogether. So his inclusion in a book on Hinduism needs a few words of justification. Krishnamurti was born in 1895 in South India. When he was nearly fourteen, he was identified by the theosophist C.W. Leadbeater as the future world teacher. Theosophists believed that Lord Maitreya (believed to be the *bodhisattva* or 'Buddha to be' in the occult hierarchy of theosophy), who had earlier incarnated as Krishna and Christ, was soon to manifest in human form. Leadbeater, who was a clairvoyant saw that Krishnamurti's psychic or astral body had no trace of selfishness, and decided that he is born thus to serve as the suitable vehicle for Lord Maitreya's arrival in the world. Later Krishnamurti was legally adopted by Anne Besant, already well-known as the founder of the theosophical movement as well as the movement for self-rule in India. From there on Krishnamurti was brought up by the Theosophical Society in the tradition of *yoga* and occultism as it then prevailed in the society.

In that tradition Krishnamurti reached the pinnacle of spirituality. As it is recorded by Mary Lutyens in her biography of Krishnamurti, *The Years of Awakening*,[47] Krishnamurti experienced the awakening of the *Kundalini Shakti* and could harness all the psychic powers that go along with it. The occult brotherhood of the Theosophical Society considered Krishnamurti to be the messiah of the new age of science and rationality. Indeed, he turned out to be the world teacher which his followers belonging to the Order of the Star (an esoteric organization within the Theosophical movement) expected him to be, but, ironically, only after his abandoning the whole theosophical movement and going along in his own way to be teaching in his most original manner his new approach to the realization of truth through self-knowing. Unlike most Hindu saints and *mahatmas* of the past,

Krishnamurti does not offer interpretations of the sacred texts of the *Vedas* and *Upanishadas*, but claims to give his own insights into the fundamentals of human existence as we know it in day-to-day life on earth. As he expounds his own understanding of spirituality in his talks and writings, it becomes abundantly clear that he is redefining some key concepts of Hinduism in a way which proves to be too maverick for the traditionalists. In particular, Krishnamurti provides a completely new understanding of God, self, living and dying, love, devotion and meditation, which in some ways tends to undermine the traditional accounts of these concepts. Furthermore, his rejection of 'disciplehood', idolatry and asceticism in the practice of religion puts him outside popular Hinduism. All the same, the focus of his teachings remains on '*moksha*' or what he calls 'the first and last freedom' which he redefines as freedom from the self, where the self in question is the familiar ego-centric consciousness philosophically known as the empirical self. Further, his belief in an 'eternal divine reality' connects him with the *Rig Veda*, and his claim that 'for freedom to be the 'I must go' connects him firmly with the Vedantic interpretation of reality as non-dualistic. So the crux of the matter is very much in keeping with the Hindu spirituality; and his own practice of locating his teachings in his own self-realization, far from being un-Hindu, in fact advances the tradition of *Gyan Marg*. The sages of the *Upanishadas* have again and again asserted what Krishnamurti has aclaimed that, 'No one can give you liberation, you have to find it within. . . . He who has attained liberation has become the teacher—like myself. It lies in the power of each one of us to enter the flame, to become the flame'.[48] He goes further to assert that in order to find this liberation 'within' no form of worship or meditation involving effort of will and asceticism can help the seeker. In the next section I will explain his own specific form of effortless meditation. And we will see that his own form of meditation is wholly consistent both with his suggestion that liberation has to be found within and that for this to happen treading the traditional paths of the organised religion is more of an hindrance than help. In saying this Krishnamurti is not denying that prayer and meditation in the traditional sense does impart some temporary calmness to the mind and consequently bestows some psychic visions and powers upon the practitioner. What he is saying is somewhat akin to Krishna's teachings that the worship of the *devas* though brings its own rewards, it does not produce spiritual enlightenment to help you to reach out to God himself. Krishnamurti is saying that in the matter of spiritual freedom any action of the will is self-defeating. Given this peculiarity of his insight, in order to grasp his own form of meditation, it is necessary to be familiar with the relevant features of his teachings in this area. For this reason, in the rest of this section I am going to present an overview of that part of his philosophy of freedom which I think will help the reader.

God: A Pathless Reality

For Krishnamurti, the reality, Truth or God or "whatever you may call it" is pathless. This central claim is the key to the understanding of his spiritual philosophy. Some academic philosophers have suggested that there is a resemblance here between Krishnamurti's ideas and the doctrines of *Theravada* Buddhism. They have then concluded that Krishnamurti simply provides a new understanding of the old Buddhism in a modern way. This conclusion is very surprising. For in view of Krishnamurti's categorical assertion of an 'eternal divine reality' which is independent of the human mind, he can by no means be compared to any major form of Buddhism or any form of Idealism. Of course, he rejects any concrete representation of this reality which in Hinduism has been subsequently done. But that again is in keeping with the *Upanishadic* spirituality rather than Buddhism. And there is a very good reason for this refrain in Krishnamurti. In every major religion of the world, as we have noted (see Ch. 2), we observe that God is spoken of in two radically different ways. On the one hand, God is thought of as 'ineffable' or beyond the grasp of the human mind, on the other hand, for the purposes of worship, he is grasped by the mind and represented in various ways in a concept which can be the focus of prayers and meditations. Krishnamurti is simply firm on one point: The ineffable must remain the 'nameless'. It is not simply a question of not representing God in a human form, any conception of a *personal* God with 'human' attributes is to drag him into the net of the mind and thereby degrade his status as a single eternal divine reality. We must be limited in our reference to God by the use of only formal notions such as 'eternal', 'divine' and 'reality' etc. God must reveal himself to the seeker. We cannot 'invite' that reality by worship or compel it by sacrifices to reveal itself. Krishnamurti explains quite convincingly why there cannot be a 'method' and consequently laid down definite pathway to that reality. By following a sect, a religion with its dogmas and rituals or a Guru, one may find whatever they lead one to, but it can never be that which is beyond thought, which is eternal and absolute.

Freedom from the Self

The awareness of the eternal spiritual realty constitutes the condition of human freedom. The inner freedom which Krishnamurti is concerned with is primarily a freedom from one's own "conditioned" nature. The psychological self made of the memories of the past experiences is identical with the total structure of the conditioned nature. From the very beginning of his life man is conditioned by his physical and social environment to obey, to believe and to follow certain traditions. The following may be necessary for learning certain facts and skills which are useful in the preservation and the acquisition of the necessities of life. But alongwith this kind of learning we also learn about our social and cultural identities, about who we are in terms of our collective history and myths and other super-natural beliefs. These identities are psychological constructs which demand that we think and feel and live our lives according to certain social ideals in certain definite ways. We are coerced into conformism and gradually lose our instinctive curiosity for truth and novelty. One succumbs to mediocrity and sublimates the creative urges which are so natural to mankind. The conditioning in our upbringing deprives us of our true individuality.

In the popular conception 'individuality' is identified with one's passion for self-fulfilment. In actual practice it boils down to 'egoistic self-assertion' of one's likes and dislikes. It is an aggressive and intolerant attitude towards others. Unfortunately, in the contemporary world which is dominated by the ideology of worldly success and consumerism, this attitude is highly prized. It is carefully cultivated in the children. But in the qualitative sense "individuality" involves norms and standards for our choices, especially the large choices which give meaning and significance to life as a whole, which refer to human freedom—a spiritual quality of the personal psychological background from which one's choices flow. But a person, who acts from the inner compulsions of his conditioned self, cannot be said to manifest that freedom. Consumed by his passion for personal success, he is steeped in his greed for 'more' and blind to the fact of his interconnectedness with life as a whole. The conditioned self lacks the background of freedom and true individuality. The "I" serves as the centre for a complex structure of personal motives which are self-directed in the sense that, although overtly they are directed towards achieving some result in the world, covertly they are aiming at 'becoming' so-and-so or such-and-such through those achievements. Thus, for example, when an artist uses his art, a musician uses his violin to become rich and famous, he is not aiming to realize the internal goodness of his art for its own sake. He is aiming at personal success. He is moved by the inner compulsion of seeking a secure status for his psychological self rather than by the joy of creativity. In this process we learn to love and hate selectively, to compare and compete in ways which give us a feeling of security. We learn to react, rather than act, to situations from a background of the conditioned 'knowledge' of ourselves—a background which is unavoidably tainted with prejudice, bias and misinformation, with propaganda and illusions about our supernatural status. Clearly this knowledge is not based on truth and our essential humanity.

We grow up into believing that each of us is a separate psychological entity which is independent of the body and which is permanent despite our constantly changing mental states. But in face of the fact that the human being, with which we are first and foremost acquainted, is necessarily dependent for its existence, both in respect of his mind and his body, upon its immediate environment, it is difficult to believe that we are essentially, ontologically, separate entities. In fact, all the evidence available points to the 'interconnectedness' of all things. Human beings tend to think that they are islands unto themselves and tend to forget that islands could never exist without the undivided land beneath the waters that surround them. Is it then that the most widely accepted view of ourselves is mistaken? Is it then that the isolation of the ego-centric self is a myth promoted by the human desire for an eternal personal existence? Krishnamurti's answer to these questions is decisively 'yes'.

Krishnamurti's position in this matter can be best understood by his explanation of how the distinction between 'me' and 'non-me' arises in the first place. This has something to do with the nature of empirical consciousness. He explains that the actual consciousness operates simultaneously at two different levels. Consider an ordinary case of sense-perception. First, there is the straightforward consciousness of an object. And then immediately there is the consciousness of this consciousness in which the object is brought under a concept. This second level of consciousness of consciousness is a response of thought or memory in which the object perceived is recognized as thus and so and evaluated. It is in this response of thought that the 'me'-'non-me' distinction arises in the first place. And later the 'me' is given a separate ontological status. Krishnamurti makes this point as follows: "So there is the superficial awareness of the tree, the bird, the door, and there is the response to that, which is thought, feeling, emotion. Now when we become aware of this response, we might call it a second depth of awareness. There is the awareness of the rose and there is the awareness of the response to the rose. Often we are unaware of this response to the rose. In reality it is the same awareness which sees the rose and which sees the response. It is one movement and it is wrong to speak of the outer and inner awareness. When there is a visual awareness of the tree without any psychological involvement there is no division in relationship. But when there is a psychological response to the tree, this response is a conditioned response, it is the response of the past memory, past experiences, and this response is a division in relationship. This response is the birth of what we shall call the 'me' in relationship and the 'non-me'. This is how you place yourself in relationship to the world. This is how you create the individual and the community. The world is seen not as it is, but in its various relationships to the 'me' of memory. This division is the life and the flourishing of everything we call our psychological being, and from this arises all contradictions and division. . . . When there is the awareness of the tree there is no evaluation. But when there is a response to the tree, when the tree is judged with like and dislike, then a division takes place in this awareness as the 'me' and the 'non-me', the 'me' who is different from the thing observed. This 'me' is the response, in relationship, of past memory, past experiences".[49] Krishnamurti further maintains that if there can be an awareness of the tree and the response to the tree without any judgement or evaluation then the principle of division, the principle of 'me' and 'non-me' will be eradicated. In such "choiceless" awareness Krishnamurti's famous slogan "you are the world" stands fully vindicated. Again, in the above philosophy of the self, one can see very clearly that Krishnamurti is advancing the *vedantic* discourse of Shankara's non-Dualism, which maintains that the Self and the Reality are ultimately one.

These conclusions can be further strengthened by the well-known facts about our bodily and mental existence. We can see that at neither of these levels our essential separateness from the world can be asserted. We know that as biological entities we have evolved from the earth, we are constantly drawing sustenance from the earth and we will eventually return to the earth. At the mental level, at first, it seems obvious that the "I" is separate from its experiences which arise in the body-brain inhabited by the "I", and each "I" is substantially distinct from other "I's". But a little reflection reveals that it is not so. At first it appears that I am the source of my experiences, that I give rise to them in some original sense, *ab initio* as it were. After all no one else suffers *my* pain and thinks my thoughts. And given that the thinker and the sufferer cannot be identified with the body, it is taken for granted that it must be a mental substance, one for each individual human being. But against this belief let us note the following facts of experience. Firstly, no one can claim a direct cognitive awareness of such a substance in one's own case or in the case of another. Next, phenomenological reflection reveals that the ego, far from being the source of 'my' stream of consciousness, is in fact an "object" of consciousness. As Krishnamurti has pointed out that the 'me' arises only when I become aware of my response to my straightforward consciousness of something. Indeed, the 'I' is always apprehended along with some or the other state of consciousness as an aspect of it under which the state in question is considered "owned". The 'owner' is never apprehended separately from the experience it is supposed to own. In actual fact the thinker is the thought; the experiencer is mingled with and spread throughout the experience. On the other hand, given that the experiences are wholly integrated in the causal network that operates in the world, it is impossible to treat them as essentially separate existences. It follows, therefore, that the 'stream of consciousness' flows in the same world where the Ganga flows, and is separate only to the extent that it is contained by its banks and only as long as it is not merged in the ocean. That is, the separateness of the self is a functionally relative matter.

It is clear then that the contents of this self, its particularity, has been acquired through the process of one's upbringing. In this process, as already noted, we not only learn certain impersonal truths and certain factual data about ourselves, we also acquire an 'emotive' identity. This emotive identity is made of our likes and dislikes, our prejudices and attachments and a whole host of titles under which we are conditioned to subsume ourselves—such as those pertaining to caste, creed, tribe, religion and nationality etc. We begin to think that one is essentially, for example, a Hindu, a Muslim or a Christian, an Indian and so on. We are then pushed into thinking, feeling and behaving in ways that are preferential to our emotive identity. Under the influence of the emotive identity our true human identity is pushed aside and conveniently forgotten.

We then tend to relate to others from the background of this emotive identity. And coupled with the belief in the essential separateness of the self (as discussed above), the focus of our relationships always remains on the 'me' and the 'I'. Our behaviour then inevitably turns out to be manipulative aiming at the satisfaction of the conditioned self.

We can see this happening even in those relationships which we identify under 'love'. In day to day life love seems to demand reciprocity. The lover wants a certain kind of attention and behavioural responses from the loved one. Indeed, he wants nothing short of being loved himself by the loved one. In frustration the lover's range of behaviour can vary from committing suicide to taking the life of the loved one itself. In the fulfilment of love we know that the lover can move mountains. He can make incredible sacrifices, while at the other end of the spectrum, he can be extremely mean and self-centered. In all these forms of behaviour the lover is being covertly self-seeking. If he is self-sacrificing it is only in order to protect his bond of attachment—an attachment without which he will feel much diminished in his own self. Generally, in love we are possessive which gives us a feeling of security. But we want to possess the other as a free person. One fails to notice the contradiction in the possessive love. One does not see that one cannot love a slave; that freedom cannot be possessed.

For Krishnamurti love is neither attachment nor possession. It is not a commodity that we can trade in or trade with. Nor it is a question of making sacrifices. Love is naturally giving and forgiving. It is not a self-conscious pursuit of virtue. When love is there the 'I' is not. It is a state of self-abandonment, a freedom from the emotive compulsions of the conditioned self. Like the perfume of a flower it is equally available to all those who would come near and have the capacity to receive it. "With one's whole being one must come upon this strange thing called love—and therefore be without fear. We mean love that is not touched by pleasure, by desire, by jealousy—love that knows no competition, that does not divide, as my love and your love. Then the mind—including the brain and the emotions—is in complete harmony".[50]

The psychology of this universal self-seeking behaviour is too complex. But Krishnamurti's insight in this matter explains it simply and most convincingly. First he observes, what has been observed by many before him, that in all his endeavours man is constantly seeking personal power, wealth or recognition in some form or the other. However, the underlying reason for this is that all these material achievements provide him a sense of psychological 'security'. There is no doubt that we need these things in some measure. But the interesting thing about this phenomenon is that we are not satisfied with that measure which is necessary for our well-being. We go on crying for more and more and in this process we go on committing a great deal of inhumanity. Indeed, in the modern world extreme forms of selfish individualism has turned even art and culture into profit-making pursuits, and institutions of learning and social service into commercial enterprises. The constancy and universality of this phenomenon of self-seeking seems to indicate that the cause of this is deep in the human condition and not necessarily connected with the lack of material resources in the world. In Krishnamurti it is connected with our belief in the nature of the self. As we have seen that we generally believe that the self is not only a separate individual entity, but also that it is unchanging and permanent. In the world of total impermanence the self is imagined to remain constant throughout its changing psychological biography. But when we look into ourselves we cannot find anything of this kind. On the other hand, in the heart of hearts we all know that death awaits us all. But we crave for permanence. Externally the world is in a state of complete uncertainty. Almost anything can happen anytime to destroy all our hopes and plans for the future. In such a situation it is only natural to feel insecure.

The self-consciousness keeps this sense of insecurity always alive. It divides and isolates my existence from the rest of being. From the very childhood we grow up with a sense of loneliness accompanying the sense of insecurity. In self-consciousness one is necessarily aware of 'not being that thing which one is aware of'. Unfortunately, in this regard our social environment is not of any help either. How could it be! After all the social environment is nothing but a projection of our inner states of conflict, uncertainty and insecurity. "We have built a society which is violent and we, as human beings, are violent; the environment, the culture, in which we live, is the product of our endeavour, of our struggle, of our pain, of our appaling brutalities".[51] The society appears to us as a challenge, an opposition to be conquered. In such a situation the individual feels alienated from the society, and the sense of insecurity continues to plague our psyche.

Now the phenomenon of constant self-seeking, which we are trying to explain is the mechanism by which we are trying to end this feeling of insecurity. We can see that the desire for power and wealth is to make us feel secure individually and not as collectively. Our psychological problem is not solved if the whole country is getting rich and powerful. Even in the most advanced nations of today, the individuals are not free from the sense of isolation and insecurity. We need these things for ourselves individually. That is why Krishnamurti maintains that 'systems' and 'revolutions' in the society cannot help us. To end the sense of insecurity we need a 'revolution within'. It is the same thing with the seeking of recognition or fame. Temporarily, it makes one feel that he is a part of a larger whole, a community. And the sense of alienation is forgotten for a while. But the individual-society relationship has not changed fundamentally. The 'I' is soon going to separate me from the rest of humanity. The insecurity due to the fact of uncertainty and impermanence is going to haunt me again. And the race for more and more power, wealth and recognition is going to continue. We will see in the next part of this writing what Krishnamurti has to offer as a permanent solution of this problem. For the moment, to complete the background for that, I turn to another theme which is most relevant here.

Freedom and the Ending of Time

Krishnamurti maintains that the freedom from the emotive self which we have been talking about amounts to a freedom from the personal past. And since without the past there is no future either, it is a freedom from time altogether. But surely time seems to be the very essence of man. Both physically and mentally one's life seems to be structured in time. Physically, the biological life of an individual has a beginning and ending in time. Like any other thing in the objective world, the body of a human being manifests growth and change which require time. A still life will be no life at all. So time seems to be a necessary feature of life. And inwardly, subjectively, we all think of ourselves as beings spread across time. Not only that we are constantly aware of a world in time, we are also aware of our very existence as a 'unity' of past, present and future. One thinks and actually remembers oneself to be a continuity in time. One does not think of oneself either as a disjointed or as a momentary self. The nature and significance of 'freedom from time', therefore, has to be properly understood. In modern philosophy generally, and existentialism particularly, temporality is seen to constitute the very essence of man, of the essence which makes him what he is. The understanding of temporality, therefore, is essential to the understanding of his humanity itself.

In this context Krishnamurti introduces a very important distinction between time in its objective reference and time as a subjective phenomenon. The former is the familiar time, the chronological time, which is measured by the watch. And Krishnamurti is under no illusion that one has to keep a count of this time if, for example, one is doing a scientific experiment or trying to win a race. In this respect time is an essential feature not only of man but of the whole of existence. In suggesting freedom from time Krishnamurti is not suggesting that we ignore the existence of the objective time. For Krishnamurti the temporality of man in question is constituted by what he calls the "psychological time". The psychological time is made of a person's consciousness of a personal past and a personal future. The personal past is made of memories and the personal future is made of his hopes and his desire for continuity. Mentally, he carries this past into the present and projects it into the future. He whole-heartedly believes in its reality. But it is clear that in reality there is no past as such, or else it will be existing now. And past could not be existing in the present. The same argument applies to the future. For anything to be real it has to be existing in the present. And future will not be 'future' if it were to exist in the present. It is memory that has created the expanse of personal time. It is the whole endeavour of man to achieve and "become" someone that has a movement in the psychological time. But we have already seen that 'becoming' is a mere illusion. It is the desire for permanence that sustains the illusion of 'becoming'. For Krishnamurti freedom from time is the freedom from the desire of permanence through 'becoming'. It is freedom from the psychological time.

We can now see that the psychological time does not constitute the essential humanity of man. The desire for continuity of the psychological self is mechanical. It is a product of conditioning, of the social environment. It does not manifest love or freedom. If anything qualifies as the essence of man as a human being, it is surely his 'creative intelligence'. The creative intelligence is holistic and characterized by the quality of spontaneity. It is creative in respect of its capacity to grasp Truth, Goodness and Beauty. The desire for continuity is insensitive to man's being for moment to moment creativity. It condemns man to the meaningless project of 'becoming' without understanding the true nature of the self. For Krishnamurti living is a movement in relationship. But when "relationship is tethered to the past, to memory, its movement is limited and becomes agonizing".[52] That is, when life is guided by the motive of 'becoming', it is being guided by the conditioned past. A self-seeking activity can only breed mischief, violence, illusions, anxiety and strife, which cannot be identified with the essential humanity of man. The psychological temporality of man is of the nature of bondage, which must be transcended. The flowering of humanity in man brings with it the true virtues of innocence, wisdom, moral courage and compassion, which are founded in freedom of being without becoming. Man can live his humanity only when there is this freedom; when love is manifest spontaneously in the absence of the 'me'.

Action and Relationship

It is in his philosophy of action that we see most clearly how

Krishnamurti pursues and advances some of the central concerns of the *Gita*. In the *Gita*, as we have seen, action has to be at once both, morally correct and spiritually propitious. Such action is founded in selflessness which is a function of non-attachment. There it is clearly stated that the right kind of action is that which is not performed with the motive of personal gain. Of course, in performing any action one is trying to achieve some result in the material world. But what is required is that one's own reason for performing that action should not be personal gain through achieving the result in question. In the same vein Krishnamurti also maintains that action with an eye on personal success is neither virtuous nor spiritual. In his rendering of the case, virtue and spirituality are both grounded in 'freedom from the self'. First with regard to virtue, Krishnamurti is clear in his mind that virtue is neither a matter of habitual action nor a matter of conscious practice of certain rules or modes of behaviour designated as virtuous. In his usual enquiring mode, Krishnamurti asks us to free ourselves from the accepted patterns of the social morality: "Can we discard the morality of society which is really quite immoral? Its morality has become respectable, approved by religious sanctions. . . . This morality is to go to war, to kill, to be aggressive, to seek power, to give hate its place; it is all the cruelty and injustice of established authority. . . . If our behaviour is directed by the environment in which we live, controlled and shaped by it, then it is mechanical and heavily conditioned. And if our behaviour is the outcome of our own conditioned response, is it moral? If your action is based on fear and reward, is it righteous? If you behave rightly according to some ideological concept or principle, can that action be regarded as virtuous? So we must begin to find out how deeply we have discarded the morality of authority, imitation, conformity and obedience".[53] Krishnamurti is enquiring into the very basis of our so-called moral action. He rightly observes that an action proceeding from the background of the conditioned self, which is a product of the environment, cannot be virtuous. Such action is more of the nature of reaction. It is the reaction of the 'emotive self' which, we have noted, is constituted by the past attachments. It is mechanical: it proceeds from the desire to seek personal security through wealth, power and recognition. But 'virtue' refers to human freedom and spontaneity which are available only in the absence of the 'me'. So truly virtuous a ion could not be those that are performed with the motive of rewards of a personal nature. In the 'non-me' there is the manifestation of love, which represents the supreme order of existence. It is the only virtue in relationship. When relationship proceeds from the background of love, it is natural and spontaneous. One does not have to mould one's moral life into a pattern. Love brings its own order, responsibility and discipline. "Order means the understanding of what disorder is and freeing the mind from that disorder—the disorder of resistance, of greed, envy, brutality and fear. And out of that freedom comes a virtue which is not something cultivated by thought. . . ."[54]

We can now see that a virtuous action is also endowed with the highest spiritual quality of transcendence. As the virtuous action is not mechanical, it is not a mere reaction, it is also not repetitive. In its beginning is its end. Though outwardly it may look similar to the one performed before and could be classified objectively, but inwardly, it is not 'owned' by the self in the sense of being held by a personal motive. Because it proceeds from the background of love, the virtuous action has that quality of newness, the freshness, which is so characteristic of creativity. This is not to say that in virtuous action one is always creating a standard aesthetic composition such as a poem or a work of art or a melody. It is rather like the same *raga* being sung on different occasions, yet each time it manifests the quality of transcendence. Indeed, the whole life of a man in whom actions proceed from the background of love is virtuous. He lives like an "artist of life". In ordinary life we are ambitious. The driving force behind ambition is always the rewards it brings. Actions based in ambition strengthen the self in the sense that the desire for 'becoming' grows stronger. Such actions are within the field of time. Even if they are religious in the standard sense, they do not manifest the spiritual quality of transcendence. But when actions are founded in selflessness they are at once both virtuous and spiritual. "Living means that every day you are abandoning everything that you are attached to. A very simple fact, but it has got tremendous implications. So that each day is a new day. Each day you are dying and incarnating. There is tremendous vitality and energy because there is nothing you are afraid of. There is nothing that can hurt. All things that man has put together have to be totally abandoned. That's what it means to die . . . Love and death go together".[55]

Next, in his psychology of action, Krishnamurti's insight offers an improvement upon the *Gita*. In the *Gita* the origin of action is in desire. But what is the origin of desire itself? Krishnamurti rightly observes that before desire there is perception, and before perception there is the mind's contact with the world. Krishnamurti maintains that it is this point of contact where action actually begins. And it is most important that we meet the world rightly. For if we do not, if we are careless right in the beginning, we cannot expect our actions either to be virtuous or spiritual. It is here that he introduces the most original notion of "observing without the observer". Ordinarily, when we observe outwardly, when we look or listen etc., our minds don't perceive things as they are. The 'What is' is not seen or heard without our interpretation of it. We immediately tend to superimpose our concept, our pre-conceived notions and prejudices upon 'What is'. We pass judgement upon it almost immediately. But the interpretation or the judgement is a conditioned response. It is a reaction of the memory. But the memory constitutes the self, the observer. As we have seen for Krishnamurti there is no separate individual called 'the observer. So in this case we are not observing without the observer. The 'I' is always present in our reactions at the very first step of our contact with the world. The result is that 'What is' is delivered in thought. But thought is always limited, partial and old. It cannot capture the living reality in all its newness and all its glory. Consequently, the mind is unable to perceive the significance of the observed reality for the 'whole'. This gives rise to wrong desire and subsequently the whole endeavour to fulfil it. The observing without the observer gives an understanding of the whole. The understanding, which is its own action, brings freedom from the compelling demands of the observed. The understanding and the freedom are not 'rewards' of the action of observing. They cannot be possessed and utilized for further 'becoming'. If we observe with the motive of reward, it will fail to produce the relevant understanding and freedom. We will have more to say about this in the next section. For the moment I wish to emphasize that 'observing without the observer' is the same type of action which the *Gita* recommends at the behavioural level—an action without the motive of personal gain. This is the essence of the philosophy of non-attachment. And Krishnamurti, by introducing a new way of observing 'What is' at the very beginning of action, makes an advancement in that philosophy. One has to begin rightly in order to end rightly.

J. KRISHNAMURTI—II

In Krishnamurti, meditation requires an existential understanding of life, in the knowledge of the ways of the operational self as it is actually implicated in the day to day life of the individual. Such knowledge involves understanding the way THOUGHT operates within the dualistic framework of subject-object relationship. For Krishnamurti to know ourselves means to know our relationship with the world. The understanding of this relationship does not demand any specialization either in the scriptures or in the sciences. What it demands is simple 'choiceless' awareness which can meet life as a whole. When one is aware, for example, of the whole process of desire in oneself, one notices that there is always an object towards which the mind is oriented for further sensation. And this process naturally involves resistance, temptation and discipline. This process is 'perception-sensation-contact-desire'. And the mind becomes 'the mechanical instrument of this process, in which symbols, words and objects are the centre around which all desire pursuits, and ambitions are built; that centre is the "me".' In Krishnamurti's meditation, which can be practised simultaneously to the conduct of daily life, one comes to understand the very basis of human relationships. One sees, for example, that the self is always self-concerned. That is, in whatever one does in actual life the self's point of view is always of "what's in it for me". It is very rare that one is aware of something or does something with deep love, without a personalised motive of some gain for oneself. Similarly, one perceives that the self is generally inclined towards the most pleasurable, avoiding calculating its effect on other people, even if it proves damaging to oneself in the long run. Thus one realizes the mechanical nature of the mind. Thoughts full of desire impel the self to move into the intentional nexus always to fulfil oneself. That is, an action is performed with simultaneously two different intentions behind it.

One is the straightforward intention to complete the job one has undertaken to do. And the other is self-reflexive. That is, by completing the job one is covertly aiming at some personal gratification. In this case completing the job is merely a means to further end of some personal gain. It is not simply or primarily for the love of the work involved. It is not like an authentic creative artist who practises his art to realize the goods internal to the art, without the directing motive of personal gain through it. He may indeed be happy at the gains he receives through it, but that would not have been his primary motive in it. Again, there are indeed many things that we do which may have no value beyond serving as means to further ends. But if that is the pattern of our human relationships, then one's life is surely mechanical and devoid of love and creativity.

In choiceless awareness, as one goes deeper and deeper into the understanding of the ways of the self, one arrives at a level of consciousness where one can take a cognitive perspective upon one's own mind, as though one were outside it. In this perspective, simultaneously to one's mental perceptions, a non-cognitive awareness of existence arises quite spontaneously, which, Krishnamurti claims, is without the 'centre', the 'I' or the ego. In this state the self experiences the limitless joy of liberation from the *karmic* order of events in which the desiring-self is implicated. One can attain this state of consciousness in this very life, and therefore, while going through the motions of *karmic* determinations until death, one is simultaneously, inwardly free from those determinations. This freedom-consciousness is manifest on a totally different dimension than the thought-consciousness. With the bodily death of the liberated self there is the total ending of thought-consciousness; and the liberated self enters the abode of the eternal, without a remainder.

Because of its familiar connotations, Krishnamurti rarely uses the word 'God'. He prefers to call it the 'Nameless', the Eternal Reality, and characterizes it as 'the source of all energy'.[56] His conception of the Nameless seems to come very close to the *Vedantic* conception of *Nirakar Brahman*, and occasionally he suggests that one may call it God if one wishes. But even to call it *Nirakar Brahman* is perhaps to make it too concrete for Krishnamurti. He takes the ineffability of God most seriously. What God is should be left open for everyone to discover for himself. And one who finds out for himself would know that God is strictly ineffable, beyond thought. The Nameless is indescribable because it is inconceivable. Thought cannot reach the true experience of God. The Nameless should not be identified with anything like the familiar attribute-bearing personal God of the theistic religions, or the Logos, or even in Shankara's way with 'Being, Consciousness and Bliss'. For Krishnamurti, one can refer to God only as the Unknown, and even the Unknowable, in so far as "knowing", in the ordinary sense, involves bringing one's intuitions under concepts. For Krishnamurti, God is simply the sacred, unknowable, Eternal Truth. But God can be accessed directly by each one of us in the silence of thought-free awareness. But such pure awareness should not be seen as emanating from an individual substantial soul. That again would be a too concrete apprehension of the spiritual-reality of the human being. Krishnamurti is content with seeing that awareness as an aspect of the human-reality which is manifest when the mind is absolutely silent.[57] For Krishnamurti, without a direct experience of this thought-free creative awareness, even the life of worldly successes and achievements is totally meaningless and devoid of any intrinsic worth.

To engage oneself, therefore, in the quest of God, the Eternal Reality, is the only truly religious endeavour. To find God is to find the unconditional freedom, the real *moksha* or *mukti*. For Krishnamurti, the ways of worship of the organised religions, involving sacrifices and self-mortification, are not truly religious, for they do not lead us to the spiritual freedom in question. Krishnamurti sees them as subtle forms of self-seeking behaviour in which, in some form or another, personal power or security is sought by invoking extra-terrestrial agencies. Moreover, the practice of worship does not transcend thought or temporality. It is fully entrenched in the computations of the mind. So religion in that sense is devoid of spirituality. True religion should not be a matter of personal, self-expansive 'achievement', even though what is to be achieved were the vision of 'God' or Heaven etc. In the quest of God one should be prepared to lose out everything with which one has identified oneself. Inwardly, one should be prepared to be 'nothing', not even the immortal individual entity called the 'soul'. Discovering God is a matter of total self-abandonment. In the quest of Truth one should not start of with any concrete idea of the soul, which is as unknown as the Nameless. In the venture of self-knowing, one should begin with the self that is knowable. This self is located in the network of relationships, with people and things, with ideals and conditioned beliefs. For Krishnamurti, one cannot exist in isolation; so 'life is relationship and relationship is action'. He considers relationship as the mirror in which one discovers himself. Indeed, without relationship one does not exist at all. Self-knowing thus involves understanding the whole of existence, not bit by bit in fragments (which will be impossible even in numerous life-times) but holistically, in an integrated self-awareness. This involves a very special kind of meditation, wholly untraditional and Krishnamurti's original. Let us see how he expounds his ideas.

Krishnamurti is a well-known critic of the popular techniques of meditation. But let us try to understand what is positive in it. His critique of the false yields a great truth concerning the traditional approaches to meditation, since 'negation is to the essence of the positive'. His analytical phenomenology suggests a unique kind of meditation. He rightly observes that the popularly available meditations teach us to concentrate on a mental image of God or a symbol and repeat certain *mantras* etc. They all involve control of consciousness through concentration on one thing or the other. When consciousness is held focused upon some particular thing for a length of time, it may indeed give you some extraordinary experiences and even release some psychic powers in you. But now, the first thing to realize is that when I have succeeded in keeping my consciousness on to one thing, I have actually managed to create a prison cell for myself. This is so because at the existential level I am identical with my consciousness. If my consciousness is encapsulated in an image or a symbol, howsoever 'holy' it may be, then I have encircled my awareness and situated myself within that mental image. How then does it help me to go beyond the mental, the concept, the language? How does it help me to transcend the familiar world of subject-object consciousness, which is the duality we live in? It will be retorted that the meditative exercises produce supra-sensible experiences. Let us say that I have a vision of Krishna. But this vision is still just a mental achievement within the temporal world of consciousness. It may be a very pleasing experience and temporarily liberating. But it doesn't seem to change things radically. It doesn't bring about a total inner transformation of my psyche. Once the effect of the experience is over, I am back to the world of my daily existence, the world of desires and the struggle to fulfil them. In meditative experiences I am still wandering on the many planes within the *sansara*. There is no freedom or *mukti* from it all. We are still living within the network of desire-struggle-hope-despair, harassed by fears of all kinds, with occasional pleasures of worldly successes. For Krishnamurti the 'spiritual' must lead us into freedom: from the temporal into the eternal, from mental struggles into creativity, from the 'I' into the universal, from prejudice and envy into the un-self-seeking totality of Love.

To accomplish this Krishnamurti suggests a meditation which is simple and straightforward. His central idea is: No concentration or control of consciousness but CHOICELESS AWARENESS of 'What is'. Choiceless awareness is the awareness of the movement of one's consciousness, without evaluation and encouragement or discouragement of the intentions and the attitudes behind these movements. It is 'silent' alongside the straightforward first-level consciousness of the world, but completely alert and attentive. In choiceless awareness one is not only aware of the manifest thoughts and feelings, but also of the so-called unconscious motives and urges which promote those thoughts and feelings. Such awareness is a unitary process which brings about a total integration of human understanding. In choiceless awareness one is able to contact the emotions of pleasure and pain directly, without the word, the thought or the idea of those emotions coming in the way. In direct contact, Krishnamurti claims, we are able to transcend these emotions and land into an extraordinary quietness and calmness of the mind. And in this way when the mind is absolutely quiet, Krishnamurti tells us, the Nameless arrives uninvited. Moreover, in choiceless awareness, one can observe the moment to moment engaged-self directly, bringing into the open its deceptions, fears and longings. Such meditation produces a deep understanding of the true nature of the self and its relation to the world. And the action of this understanding frees the mind from the conditioned urges to seek an impossible permanence and security for the self, in a world of total impermanence and endless uncertainty. "It is like leaving the window open and the air comes when it will—whatever the air brings, whatever the breeze is. But if you expect, wait for the breezes to come because you have opened the window, they will never come. So it must be opened out of love, out of affection, out of freedom—not because you want something. . . . To be aware is an extraordinary state of mind—to be aware of your surroundings, of the trees, the bird that is singing, the sunset behind you; to be aware of the faces, of the smiles; to be aware of the dirt on the road; to be aware of the beauty of the land, of a palm tree against the red sunset, the ripple of the water—just to be aware, choicelessly. . . . In that state of awareness there is attention—not control, not concentration. . . . Concentration is exclusion. . . . If you concentrate, you merely resist, exclude. But a mind that is attentive can concentrate and not be exclusive. So out of this attention comes a brain that is quiet. . . . The brain must be very quiet, because without quietness—uninduced, not brought about artificially—there can be no clarity. . . . So the mind becomes completely still, without any form of pressure, compulsion. This stillness is not a thing produced by thought because thought has ended, the whole machinery of thought has come to an end . . . you have to understand this whole machinery of thought, not how to stop thinking . . . if you understand it, naturally it comes to an end. When the mind is completely still, then out of that stillness, in that stillness, there is quite a different movement".[58]

So if one could keep oneself choicelessly aware, attentive to the whole movement of life, then, Krishnamurti claims, that there will be a total inner transformation. And in that transformation the seeker of God is made fit to receive the eternal. "If the mind has gone that far, that movement is creation. That state of mind that is in that complete silence—it will move, it has its own movement into the unknown, into that which is unnameable".[59] In the movement of the eternal there is liberation, there is *moksha*, the first and last FREEDOM. The moment to moment sustenance of the spontaneity of personal being-consciousness is itself an indication of the presence of that creative energy behind the ego. Krishnamurti shows us the way to put aside the 'me' and allow the creative energy to guide our lives in total spiritual freedom.

REFERENCES

1. *Gita*, 6, 1-2.
2. Pt. I, 1.
3. 1, 34-6.
4. 5, 27-28.
5. *Gita*, 6, 8.
6. *Ibid.*, 6, 10.
7. Ch. 18, 45-46.
8. *Gita*, Ch. 16, 12-14.
9. X, 129, 4.
10. Ch. 3, 5.
11. *A Source Book in Indian Philosophy*, ed., Radhakrishnan and Moore, Princeton, 1967, p. 248 and *Gita*, Ch. 1, 31.
12. 1, 32.
13. Ch. 2, 47.

14. Ch. 15, 5.
15. *Gita*, Ch. 3, 30.
16. Ch. 3, 13.
17. Ch. 3, 19.
18. Ch. 4, 20.
19. 4, 22.
20. Ch. 9, 9.
21. Ch. 12, 6, 7.
22. *Gita*, 6, 30.
23. *Rigveda*, 8, 16, 11.
24. *Gita*, 10, 10-11.
25. *Ibid.*, 4, 39-40.
26. *Ibid.*, 18, 61-62.
27. *Op cit.*, 65-66.
28. *Op cit.*, 54.
29. *Op cit.*, 56.
30. *Gita*, 6, 47.
31. *Gita*, 14, 1.
32. *Ibid.*, 12, 13.
33. *Ibid.*, 15, 5.
34. *Ibid.*, 7, 16-19.
35. *Op cit.*, 23-25.
36. *Shvetashvatara*, 3, 7.
37. *Gita*, 7, 14.
38. *Ibid.*, 2, 59.
39. *Ibid.*, 4, 37-38.
40. 10, 8, 38.
41. 7, 29.
42. Osborne A. (edited), *The Collected Works of Ramana Maharshi*, published by T.N. Venkataraman, Sri Ramanabramam, Tiruvannamalai, S. India, 1974, p. ii.
43. *Ibid.*
44. *Op cit.*, p. 45.
45. *Op cit.*, p. 65.
46. *Op cit.*, pp. 13-14.
47. For a brief summary of this book see her *Krishnamurti: The Years of Fulfilment*, Avon Books, U.S.A., 1984, Ch. 1.
48. Cf. *ibid*, p. 13.
49. *The Second Penguin Krishnamurti Reader*, ed., Mary Lutyens, U.K., 1972, p. 165.
50. *Beyond Violence*, B.I. Publications, New Delhi, 1984, p. 88.
51. *Ibid.*, p. 75.
52. *The Second Penguin Krishnamurti Reader*, p. 139.
53. *Ibid.*, p. 210.
54. Krishnamurti, *You are the World*, KFI, Madras, 1987, p. 151.

55. Krishnamurti, *The Last Talks*, KFI, 1992, p. 93.
56. Lutyens, M., *Krishnamurti: The Years of Fulfilment*, Avon Books, N.Y., 1984, p. 237.
57. Krishnamurti, J., *The Last Talks*, Krishnamurti Foundation India, 1992, p. 99.
58. Krishnamurti, J., *On God*, Krishnamurti Foundation India, 1999, pp. 94-97.
59. *Op. cit.*, p. 97.

8

EPILOGUE

Hinduism rightly contemplates that man is essentially a spiritual entity, that there is much more to life than what meets the eyes. So materialism and its cognate 'consumerism' can never be the answer to any of the fundamental dilemmas and paradoxes of life. Basically, human life is seriously caught up in the dilemma of nursing self-interest against the more charitable view of nursing the ideal of giving equal importance to the interest of all others, of living up to the *Vedic* ideal of '*vasudhaiva kutumbkum*' or 'the mankind is one family'. But the *Gita* with its philosophy of 'action without the motive of personal gain' has provided the final solution to the dilemma.

It was a great social tragedy that in India 'caste', which was originally meant to be simply a recognition of the already existing ethnic diversity for a peaceful coexistence, became hierarchical and enforced the unwisdom of each group's sticking to its so-called 'own' profession and vocation from generation to generation. This has no sanction of the Hindu spiritual scriptures. Only some corrupt vested interests have advocated the hierarchical order in latter secondary religious literature. Indeed, on the contrary, the *Gita* refers to the earlier meaning of 'caste' and states that 'a Brahmin is one who is by his own natural disposition inclined to lead a life of piety and spiritual quest'. Similarly, a Shudra is one 'who is naturally disposed to be in the service of others'; a Vaishya is 'naturally drawn to farming and trading', and a Kshatriya to 'power, governance and charity' (ch. 18, 41-44).

The *Gita* resolves all conflicts of interest between oneself and others by invoking the supreme ethical principle of 'impartiality' and by making a judicious adherence to it a necessary condition of receiving the grace of God (ch. 18, 54). Further, in the *Gita*, Krishna makes it absolutely clear that He leads all those to *moksha* who take refuge in Him, irrespective of caste and gender, and even the sinners who turn to Him (ch. 10, 32).

Most important of all, however, is the *Gita*'s radical solution to the central paradox of existence at the very heart of the human-reality: the paradox of 'being through becoming'. Both in his mental and physical existence the *being* of man is a constant process of becoming. Through a constant process of change, one is never the same from moment to moment. Yet, one is also constantly aware of the abiding sameness of one's 'self' continuing from birth to death, throughout one's changing biography. The 'becoming' is subject to causality but the Self, through its will and its capacity for creativity, seems always to be free. Human life is menaced by this paradox and harassed by the threat of causality. It is to the extreme credit of Hinduism that it shows us the way to removing the illusion of our subjection to causal determination by realizing the true nature of the human soul, and by locating the true and ultimate goal of human life in the quest of the eternal 'freedom-in-God'.

It is also because of 'freedom' as the focus of Hinduism that, in actual practice, it is so unfettered by the commandments of an organised religion. Hinduism is least 'organised' in the sense that it has no central (even decentralized) authority in matters of interpretation of Truth and morality. Hinduism is an open 'source book' of the highest authentic, religious, spiritual and moral experiences of the passionate seekers of Truth. One can delineate one's particular strand of faith according to one's own wisdom. At this, one is reminded of Gandhi's remark, when questioned about his respect for other faiths, that he was a good Muslim and a good Christian because he was a good Hindu.

INDEX